# Pra

## *It's time to*
## WRITE YOUR DAMN BOOK, WOMAN!

"I experienced a wealth of inspiration as part of Lyndsie's FemAuthors group, and this book mirrors that same magic! Thanks to Lyndsie's guidance, I turned my book idea into a reality, now available on Amazon and in a local Indigo store. Her writing tips, book roadmap, and checklists are trusty companions on your journey to becoming a published Author. You'll also dive into her Author journey and the stories of the women she's worked with. Get ready to unleash your inner writer - this book is the spark you've been waiting for!"

~ Tiana Fech, MEd, Learning Development Consultant and Author of **Online Course Creation 101**

"Embracing Fempreneur Marketing School, then the FemAuthors group, are two of the best decisions I made for my business. The wisdom and techniques in this book helped me become an Author AND develop highly effective marketing skills and *priceless* connections."

~ Noreen Music, Professional Organizer and Author of **The Unexpected Entrepreneur**

"Becoming a Speaker and Author seemed daunting until I met Lyndsie. She walked me through building an online presence and along the way introduced me to many kind and encouraging Fempreneurs. Lyndsie's ability to meet you wherever you're at is phenomenal. Her passion for helping women live up to their potential is in every page of this book."

~ Cynthia Hamilton Urquhart, Retired RCMP Member, Speaker and Author of **A First Responder Voice**

This book is an invaluable resource in figuring out who my book will for, how to market it and how to *actually* get it done. I love how the *doable* action steps are laid out in sequential milestones. As I read, I feel like Lyndsie is here in my corner start to finish. I now have the tools and accountability to finish my damn book!"

~ Chris Swail, Life and Health Coach at **alittlebitbetter.ca**

WRITE YOUR DAMN BOOK, WOMAN!  BY LYNDSIE BARRIE

*Other books by Lyndsie Barrie:*

Money & The 39 Forever Mom

Find Your Voice On Social Media

We Should Be Friends

Fempreneur Marketing School Workbook

The Fempreneur's Leadership & Marketing 90 Day Action Plan

Check out Lyndsie's marketing school and other programs at yycfempreneurs.com.

WRITE YOUR DAMN BOOK, WOMAN!   BY LYNDSIE BARRIE

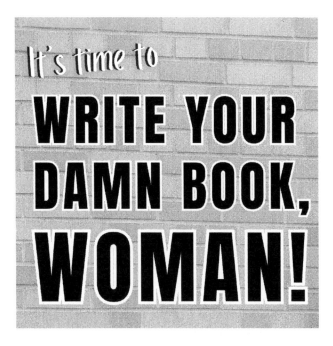

## LYNDSIE BARRIE

Copyright © 2024 Lyndsie Barrie
Published by Barrie Financial Consulting Inc.

Collaborators: Carey Wilkinson Lee, Noreen Music,
Felicia Yap and Tiana Fech

Request permission to reproduce parts of this publication, other than brief quotations, at yycfempreneurs.com/contact

Cover photos by Camille Elain (front) and Viry Escobar (back)
Cover and interior design by Lyndsie Barrie
Edited by Lauren Haugrud, Vera Ilnyckyj, Chris Swail,
Laurie Lakeman, Carol Reynolds and Kym Jarvis

WRITE YOUR DAMN BOOK, WOMAN!   BY LYNDSIE BARRIE

# DEDICATION

For the woman who made me the confident woman I am today.

Thanks mom.

I love you.

# DISCLAIMER

This book is not intended to serve as legal or financial advice. The strategies and concepts contained herein may not be suitable for your situation. Neither the publisher, nor the author shall be liable for any loss of profit or any other commercial damages.

# CONTENTS

| | |
|---|---|
| I'm not gonna sugar coat it | 11 |
| 1. How to get started writing a book | 17 |
| 2. How to not quit | 35 |
| 3. Before we hit the road, let's look at the map | 51 |
| 4. Get in the PURPLE zone | 73 |
| 5. Knowledge is powerless without ACTION | 103 |
| 6. Everything you need to know about marketing your upcoming book | 137 |
| 7. Edit, beautify & STOP | 155 |
| BONUS CHAPTER: Party Planning | 165 |
| About The Author | 175 |

WRITE YOUR DAMN BOOK, WOMAN!  BY LYNDSIE BARRIE

# I'm not gonna sugar-coat it

If you do not write a book your impact on this world will be less than it should be.

It's obvious you feel called to write a book or you wouldn't be holding this one in your hands right now! A huge congrats to you for taking this first and most important step!

*(Is this book a little skinnier than you would expect a book about writing a book to be? I hope so!)*

Mixed in with my blueprint for writing a book you'll find inspiring stories and writing tips from four women who recently wrote their first book: Carey Wilkinson-Lee, Noreen Music, Felicia Yap and Tiana Fech.

The reason I wrote this book is **becoming an Author changed my life in more ways than I could have ever imagined.** Doors opened. My confidence soared. Amazing people found me. My income grew. All because I wrote that damn book!

In 2014 I hired a business coach after hearing him speak at an event. The stories he shared about his life on stage made me feel a connection to him. I could relate to him. Ultimately that feeling of connection and his relatability were what made me TAKE ACTION. Ten years earlier he had similar goals to mine. When I met him, he had the blueprint to achieving those goals - and I wanted it!

But there is more to why I hired him so quickly...

In addition to his relatability, it was because he wrote a book - a few books, actually. I immediately viewed him with a higher regard. He became a bigger deal in my mind. Then he described how becoming an Author impacted his career and I felt like he was talking directly to me - like there was no one else in the room.

I remember feeling like, *"Lyndsie, this door that has opened for you. All you need to do is walk through it and you can enjoy all the success this man is describing on the other side."* It was like on the TV show "Queen of The South" when Teresa Mendosa's future self appears in a white suit, looking all successful and rich, to help her make sense of an opportunity or course correction.

As I sat in that conference room surrounded by 100 other Financial Advisors, I clearly saw a glimpse of my future: soon I would be on stage inspiring women to get out of their comfort zones so they could experience more fulfillment and financial stability.

I knew that version of me was inside, waiting to emerge.

**Important note:** Becoming an Author wasn't even on my radar. I had thought about writing a slightly embellished novel about my life growing up, but never a "How-To" or "Self-Help" book. I always loved writing. In elementary school I loved adding big words to my vocabulary which my parents didn't use. My teachers in often complimented me on my writing. I journaled almost every night before bed. I got a kick out of writing my re-enactments of interactions with boys I had a crush on and fights with my parents.

Imagining people's reactions to each sentence, my writing goal was humour over truth. Later, I thought about turning my years of journal entries into a funny memoir, but it seemed like too much work.

I became a mom and "adulting" became my focus. I exchanged my creativity for money to pay my bills, which became less and less fun.

Hearing and understanding the impact becoming an Author would have on my life gave me a huge surge of creativity and excitement. Sharing my "adulting" wisdom related to finance *with humour* - I'm in!! I could already feel the book starting to create itself in my soul. Writing a book went from something I could do to something I was 100% committed to doing.

Would I have decided to hire my first business coach or write my first book that day without the man on stage sharing his real and raw life story?

No.

## Don't discount the power of your stories, woman!

The best social media marketing posts, blogs and YouTube videos include a story. And all the most impactful self-improvement or professional development books include tons of compelling, relatable stories.

How many times have you felt inspired to do something bold and brave because you heard a story about someone who did it? It's a fact: stories create lasting change and fulfillment in people's lives.

It's our job as entrepreneurs and writers to share stories from our personal lives to attract the right people - those who <u>need</u> the positive change we have to offer.

***Telling people what to do with steps and stats does not evoke the emotional reaction required for making lasting positive change.***

That's why herein you'll find real and raw stories from us - Carey, Noreen, Felicia,Tiana and me. We want to encourage you to *write your damn book, woman!*

## Women inspiring women

While writing my first book, my life improved BIG TIME. Before my book was even complete I was already experiencing financial and credibility benefits because I followed the marketing system in this book: I set up and grew a niche email list, provided "natural next steps" for how to become my client, became an international speaker, and built new income streams.

Then, after my book was complete, more financial and credibility benefits came.

Everything I gained was awesome, but what was even more awesome was inspiring other women to do and be more.

During the nine months it took me to write my first book, many people were watching what I was doing. Some I've had the pleasure of meeting and some I'll never know. People reached out to me asking how I got started writing my book. Their questions were usually about technical matters, like how to design a book cover or who edited the book for me. Seeing someone write a book, a goal they once thought was too difficult, gave them the confidence to pursue it.

However, not everyone cheered me on or asked me for writing tips.

As you reach higher and higher levels of success, certain people in your world (some you don't even know) will try to pull you back into your comfort zone or knock you down. It's actually a sign that you are moving in the right direction, so when it happens, celebrate it! Trolls, haters and negative family members will appear, and when they do, remember that their limiting beliefs are NOT FOR YOU. And that their issues are NOT ABOUT YOU.

Keep focusing on the women who inspire you and know that you are inspiring women to live better lives.

## Six big gold nuggets

Even though my marketing efforts were resulting in hundreds of new LinkedIn followers and email subscribers, I didn't stop to analyze why. Thanks to a handful of local "Fempreneurs" who were curious about how I was coming up with my marketing ideas, I reverse-engineered what I had done. I found six big gold nuggets. They are included in this book and are also available as a six week program called "Fempreneur Marketing School". If you'd like to learn more go to yycfempreneurs.com/fms.

The first two marketing success principles are:

1.  build a like-minded accountability team,

2.  use social media to strike up conversations with the right people.

If the idea of marketing your book makes you want to run away, read this next paragraph:

Having a team of women who are also writing and marketing books by your side is a game changer. I don't actually know anyone who has written a book without at least one writing partner. That's why I offer a "support group" called FemAuthors. You can learn about it at yycfempreneurs.com/femauthors.

## Before we begin, do this:

Picture your readers, let's say five of them, all reading the last page of your book and answer these questions:

▶ *How do you want them to feel about their new skills and knowledge?*

▶ *How do you want them to feel about you?*

Write on a new page in your notebook what you want them to understand and feel in their soul as they read the last page of your book. Later you will rip this page out of your notebook and put it on your goal board.

# Chapter One:
# How to get started writing a book

The only way to get started is JUST START WRITING, WOMAN!

Here are a few writing tips and tricks to keep in mind:

- Finding the right time and place to write will constantly evolve, so don't overthink it or over-schedule your life around writing. Try writing in different places and at different times of the day.

- You must have 2-3 hour writing timeblocks in your calendar 2-3x a week. If the creativity juices are flowing, it's great to write for more than 3 hours at a time, but only if you take a quick movement break every hour.

- When I feel inspired to write (and when I'm not driving) I STOP, DROP AND WRITE! Even if I'm sitting at a coffee shop with a friend or client, or on the phone with my mom, I grab my notebook or open Google Docs on my phone and jot down my thoughts. It's also a good idea to sleep with a notebook and pen beside your bed.

## When will you write?

While writing my first book I found the best time to get massive amounts of writing done was during the night when everyone else was sleeping. I would start sipping instant coffee and writing at 9 or 10pm. After a few hours I'd hit the wall (the words stopped flowing), but I couldn't sleep until I had a hot bath or read a book (nothing too exciting and definitely not a self-help book!). I'd sleep for a few hours, feed my son breakfast, take him to school, complete daily tasks for my financial company, take a nap, pick him up from school, and do it all over again.

Writing during "business hours" didn't work for me because I didn't have the boundaries I have now. I thought it was my job to immediately answer phone calls and respond to emails from my financial clients. This made writing during the day impossible - too many distractions.

I shared my night owl writing story with you so you don't feel crazy. Writing and marketing a book is going to require you to get outside of your comfort zone DAILY. It might mean writing late at night or getting up at 4am to write for 3 hours before you have to turn on mom-mode. You might take up power-napping (it's an amazing skill everyone should learn, in case you haven't mastered it yet!). All of this will likely cause your family or friends to worry about you and say things that seem caring, but are major downers.

No matter what they say or how they look at you, DO WHAT YOU GOTTA DO.

You're not crazy, you're just different. And that's a really good thing.

When you think about me sipping instant coffee at night, please remember this:

I DID NOT ENJOY THE TASTE OF INSTANT COFFEE. I drank it because it was a quick and cheap way to get a jolt of energy.

We all have to make sacrifices to achieve our dreams.

My dream was to write a book that would help moms feel more confident and educated about money matters so they could feel less stressed and lead their kids by example.

## Who is your book for?

My first book was/is for moms aged 39 and over. I was 33 when I wrote it. You may be wondering why the heck I decided to write a book for 39+ moms when I was only 33. It's because my business coach helped me discover my niche: *moms aged 39 and over who wanted more from their financial advisors.*

Here's what is on the back of my first book, Money & The 39 Forever Mom:

*Successful moms often don't get the financial coaching they need.*

*They know the cost of making mistakes, or not being heard. That is exactly why most of my clients are successful moms who needed more from their financial advisors.*

*As well as seeking the best opportunities for themselves, moms care deeply about the success of their children. They know what an advantage it is for their children to have access to professional financial coaching as early as possible.*

*My passion for sharing easy to understand financial knowledge with young adults and teenagers is a huge part of why I wrote this book. Every mother wants the comfort of knowing her children will be successful stewards of their money.*

I discovered my niche when my business coach asked me to think about my favourite one or two clients. They were both successful, smart, hard-working moms in their late forties who were divorced. Their husbands had been in charge of the finances. They had felt ignored and confused during meetings with their previous financial advisor. They liked working with me because I made them feel safe to ask questions and I listened to them. I enjoyed working with 39+ moms more than most of my male clients because we had more in common.

Once I knew who I was writing my book for, my next homework assignment was:

"Build a survey to get to know your niche people better." I'll walk you through this simple yet POWERFUL exercise soon.

If you own a business, choose to write your book for your favourite client or customer. Choose the people who are grateful to have you in their lives, the ones who rave about you to their friends because of a specific problem you helped them solve.

Deciding what to say on social media to attract your ideal clients is exactly the same as deciding who to write your book for:

**Your message must be crystal clear.**

**Food for thought:** *Consider writing the book you needed 5-10 years ago, especially if that's the type of person you love working with most.*

For example, when I was writing a book to help "39 Forever Moms" better understand the world of investments and financial planning, I was also writing the book I wish I had read when I was 10 years younger.

Another example is **The 4-Hour Work-week** book by Tim Ferriss. He says it's a compilation of mindsets, research findings and stories he wished he'd learned sooner, preferably in a book. Tim Ferriss often refers to himself as a "Human Guinea Pig" because he has tried so many new things, many of which did not go so well, and he shares all the details to help others get the answers faster and to avoid his mistakes.

In 2019 I wrote my second book, this time about marketing for female entrepreneurs. It shares my best marketing short-cuts; the processes I've distilled by trial-and-error.

After writing my second book I felt called to help a few women write their own books. While teaching a marketing class online I mentioned I would love to help anyone who wanted to bring their book to life. Carey Wilkinson-Lee raised her hand, and six months later her book baby was born.

Following **Carey's tips for becoming an Author** on the next page there is an exercise to help you decide who your book is for.

## Tips for Becoming An Author from Carey Wilkinson-Lee

Carey, how did it feel to complete your book?

*It was the first time I truly felt proud of myself. It still feels fabulous to know I did it, and I would love to do it again if I could discipline myself enough!*

How did you celebrate the completion of your book?

*I made a conscious effort to FEEL the success in my body. To really let myself feel what 'proud' feels like. I called my book 'How to Get out of an Abusive Relationship (with yourself)' because I wasn't used to my brain being kind to me. Finishing writing my first book was an AMAZING opportunity to let my brain celebrate our once-in-a-lifetime achievement. Then, I threw a Party (or 4... ) with contributors to my writing journey, supportive friends and family and planned a book signing at a local shop.*

### Tell us a story about one of the best connections you made because of your book and how it has helped your career.

*It was really cool when people from my past started to reach out because they saw or heard I wrote a book. There were two people in particular who I worked with at a marketing firm over 15 years ago. Together we created a workshop to deliver to students who are training to become caregivers. This was a huge perk that came from writing my book I never saw coming.*

### How has becoming an Author improved your business?

*For me, it's completely different. I decided to go back to school to learn about how an ADHD diagnosis affects people and become an ADHD Coach. I definitely use my book as a tool. I refer to it often and love to gift it to clients and others I meet who show interest in my words. I know the book will continue to positively impact my professional and personal life for my lifetime.*

### How is your personal life different now that you're an Author?

*I often refer to myself as 'Pre-book Carey' and 'Post-book Carey'. The book writing journey was completely life changing - it elevated my self esteem. I let go of a lot of the baggage I was holding - I left it in the book.*

## Carey's Top 5 Tips for completing a book:

1. *Find your most awesome workspace! I thought mine was at home for the longest time. One day, because I was waiting for someone and not at home, I wrote in a coffee shop. It was a WAY better place for me to be creative and productive.*

2. *Schedule writing timeblocks of 2 hours minimum! For me, it would take at least 30 minutes to get sorted, log on, find where I wanted to start and get in the flow. I would book 4 hour blocks (which Lyndsie advised me to guard like a newborn babe) and give them their own color in my calendar (I chose purple).*

3. *Witness your creative journey with curiosity, not judgement. Writing a book, especially a personal story, can bring up a whole lot of emotional stuff. I found taking time to recognize and process all that came up was a huge book writing bonus!*

4. *More book writing BONUS MAGIC comes when you enjoy the process and accept that it looks different for every writer. It is such a unique time to be alone with yourself and sort through who you have been, who you are and who you want to become. Embrace the magic and self-discovery!*

5. *Deadlines! Reward yourself when you meet a deadline on time.*


Lastly, what was one of the most difficult parts of writing your book?

*Just starting was hard! And I also put a lot of pressure on myself (huge stress) to create an amazing, life-changing book. This pressure stopped the creative process in its tracks many times for me. Once I was finally able to get myself into the mindset of sharing my story, I was able to write about what was most impactful for me in my life and worry less about offending or hurting someone I care about with my words. I am an avid historical fiction reader and I didn't have much experience with self-help books. It was hard to fight the feeling of being a bit of a fraud. However, eventually, I just decided to go rogue and write a book my way - without any of the rules which constantly bombard us.*

Lyndsie here again. I hope you find Carey's stories and tips about writing a book helpful.

One thing that Carey and I discovered was she had two books she wanted to write. Each book would need to be written for a different reader.

Whenever she wasn't sure about whether to add something to the book or leave it out, I asked her:

"Does this belong in book #1 or book #2?"

The answer to this became clear after we narrowed down specifically who each book was for. This is done by writing a **Book Purpose Sentence:**

This book helps (who)

learn/do (what they'll learn/do)

so they can (their desired outcome)

When we weren't sure if something belonged in book #1 or book #2, we consulted Carey's book purpose sentences:

### Carey's Book #1 Purpose Sentence:

This book helps self-critical people

discover their strengths and break the habit of negative self-talk

so they can become their own #1 fan and live a happier life.

### Carey's Book #2 Purpose Sentence:

This book helps people with ADHD

better understand their brain's unique wiring and

how to use ADHD as a SUPERPOWER.

The example on the next page is from my "Fempreneur Marketing School" workbook.

**THIS WORKBOOK HELPS** *perfectionistic Fempreneurs*

**LEARN HOW TO** *stop over-thinking their social media posts and how they look and sound in videos*

**SO THEY CAN** *attract the right clients and earn more money from their talents.*

## Write your "Book Purpose Sentence":

This book helps (who)


learn/do (what they'll learn/do)


so they can (their desired outcome)

If you are still not sure who you want to write a book for, it's likely because you have two or more different "niches" you want to write books for. Like Carey, you will have to pick <u>one</u>.

If you don't have a business coach or a mentor who is an entrepreneur, ask 5-6 of your entrepreneur friends to choose which book they think you should write first. Complete the "Book Purpose Sentence" for each book idea and then share them with your people to find out which book to write first.

If you need help with discovering your niche and clarifying your message, continue reading and completing the action steps in this book. However, my goal for this book is <u>not</u> to help people figure out who to write a book for. You need to know specifically who you're talking to each time you sit down to write. Here's why:

## If you're talking to everyone, you're talking to no one.

Once you know who you're writing for, the only thing that matters is that you **continue to write.**

New writers often compare themselves to other writers who have been writing for decades. If you find yourself doing this, here's the pep-talk you will give yourself (fold over this page so it's ready when you need it):

## "First, this is my first book. There will be more. Second, the only way to get better at writing is by putting out 'good enough' and getting feedback."

What I have loved most about writing a new book every other year and revising my past books is seeing the improvements in my writing. As time goes on I am learning how to be a more descriptive writer. I am learning how to say more with fewer words by choosing words that pack more punch.

However, this is your first book, so give your sentence composition and word choices VERY LITTLE THOUGHT.

## Get your thoughts on the page

When I was almost done writing my first book, I was shocked when I went back and read the first chapter. It had been a few months since I had written the first chapter and my writing had improved so much! I was excited, but also frustrated because I ended up re-writing the entire first chapter, which was time I wanted to put into layout and formatting. I fell a little more behind schedule when I saw the second chapter also needed more work!

Thank God for the Tim Ferriss Show Podcast episode I heard around that time: Tim said I needed to STOP. Just stop reading and making changes to my book and **hand it over to the editors.** But once I had their feedback, and implemented their changes, I found myself making more changes.

Having a book launch party scheduled will help you avoid the mistake of not stopping. Having a book launch party has been a priceless part of the book wiring process for me because I have to stick to a deadline. I have to STOP writing and making changes to my writing.

In conclusion, when I decided my book was DONE, more of my precious time was invested in getting the book noticed by those who need it rather than nit-picking it to death.

## The shopping cart approach

You don't have to WOW your readers on every single page. And besides, every reader will be WOWed by different parts of your book. Your readers will take the shopping cart approach as they read, just like we all do when we're grocery shopping, or attending a conference. We listen to each speaker just as though we were walking down each aisle at the grocery store. *We put what we need in the shopping cart and leave what we don't need.* We don't expect every item in the grocery store to be something we need or want, nor do we find everything a speaker says to be WOW-worthy.

So like I said, just get your thoughts on the page. Don't try to write a bestseller or allow yourself to believe it's even possible for your first book to be a bestseller. The pressure that comes with such thoughts will crush your dream to write a book. Avoid the pressure by staying focused on the fact that writing this book will boost your confidence and allow you to serve more of the right people.

## Speak instead of write

Is your spelling and grammar at a grade four level? You can still write a professional and impactful book. How? By speaking into the voice recorder on your phone and uploading the audio files to a transcription website like www.podse.io. Then ask five or six people who have better spelling and grammar skills than you do to edit your transcribed audio.

## How to become a more descriptive writer

Do you find yourself using plain, boring words like "nice" and "good" too often? For Heaven's sake, mix it up! Find more exciting words to describe your thoughts. Attach feelings and uplifting or funny stories to the outcomes you are helping your readers achieve.

If you find yourself using the same word over and over again to describe something, pop it into a Google search.

For example, I've been using the word "interesting" too often lately:

Now you know how to keep your audience engaged by mixing up the way you describe things. Next I want to bring your attention to something I used to struggle with: flow.

This is what I mean by "flow":

## The flow from one topic to the next

Think of "flow" like "connecting the dots" from one topic to another. When I'm trying to connect the dots for my readers, I think of a personal story that provides a "segue" into the next topic.

*By the way, "segue" is Italian for "it follows". It was originally used to describe a seamless transition between pieces of music.*

**Here's an example of a "segue":** Right now I want to move on from sharing writing tips to the mindset of becoming an Author. This is the segue I have written to connect the topics:

When your book is complete, it won't matter how many more descriptive words you could have chosen, or that a few topics could have flowed better. All that will matter is your book is complete and you can take a selfie with it and post it all over social media with the link to buy it on Amazon.

## The letters beside your name

Maybe you already have a few letters beside your name. No matter how many credentials you already have, there will be more letter added to your name very soon...

# A U T H O R.

There is only one way to get these six letters beside your name:

## WRITE YOUR DAMN BOOK, WOMAN!

Success is yours when your first book is available on Amazon. That's it. That's when you get to add "Author" to your name, and it stays there forever.

Success does NOT come from having 10/10 of your closest friends and family read and give you an A+ on your manuscript.

Success does NOT come from having the prettiest book cover or website.

Success does NOT come from having a book that has more words than what's-her-face's book who's in your industry.

**Success DOES come to those who complete the 12 milestones in this book.**

***If you're as impatient as I am, feel free to see how fast you can complete the 12 milestones!

WRITE YOUR DAMN BOOK, WOMAN!  BY LYNDSIE BARRIE

# Chapter Two:

# How to not quit

You can't quit if you don't start.

If you can't or won't commit to do these 10 things, don't start:

**The ten *commitments* of writing a book:**

1.  Schedule 2-4 hour writing timeblocks at least 3x/ week.

2.  Guard your writing time like it's your newborn baby.

3.  Write on a piece of paper the top 5 reasons why you will not quit, put the paper in a frame on your desk and read the "5 reasons why I won't quit" whenever you feel stuck or uninspired.

4.  Book a photo shoot as soon as you begin writing your book to ensure you will have professional photos which people have not seen before for marketing your book. And you will be prepared to put an awesome new photo of yourself on your book cover.

5.  Know specifically who your reader is and how your book will improve their life.

6.  Use Google Docs (docs.google.com) to record your marketing ideas, topics/lessons you want to include in your book, and to share book content with your editors.

7.  Take your growing audience along on your book writing journey using the amazing free tool we all know and love: SOCIAL MEDIA! Use the weekly social media checklist in chapter 3 to consistently show up with purpose on social media.

8.  If being in videos scares you, complete the one hour video marketing course at yycfempreneurs.com/author.

9.  Choose wisely the 5 people you spend the most time with. Make sure they are cheering you on toward the book finish line. If you need to level up "your 5 people", consider joining the FemAuthors Writing Community at yycfempreneurs.com/femauthors.

10. Use this checklist each time you sit down to write…

# WRITING TIMEBLOCK CHECKLIST

- [ ] Put your phone in airplane or silent mode in another room or with the screen facing down - no audio or visual notifications.

- [ ] Write what you feel inspired to write. Don't try to organize your thoughts or pick up where you left off at your last writing session. Just get your thoughts and ideas out, or use your "Essential Topics" for inspiration.

- [ ] If you feel stuck, re-read the Ten Commitments of Writing A Book. If any have not been done yet, TAKE ACTION!

- [ ] Set your timer for one hour. When the timer goes off, move for 5 minutes to get fresh oxygenated blood into your brain. Perhaps switch between slow squats and push ups from your knees. End your movement break by saying this mantra aloud, or another one that gets you fired up:

**MY SKILLS AND KNOWLEDGE ARE VALUABLE. I HAVE A MORAL OBLIGATION TO SHARE WHAT I KNOW WITH THE WORLD.**

# Are You All-In?

### Circle your answer: Yes / No

Congrats on circling "Yes".

## Feeling terrified is normal

As I plugged away writing my first book, I jumped back and forth between feeling more confident and smart than ever before and feeling terrified to share my bold opinions and how-to steps with people. I was on an emotional roller coaster and it took me a while to settle into feelings of faith and peace. Feeling terrified is normal in the beginning, but you can overcome it.

Writing a book forces you to take a stand, to state what you truly believe in. Gathering all those thoughts and presenting them to the world is terrifying when you think thousands of people will read your book.

But calm down. Don't tell yourself that thousands (or tens of thousands) of people will be reading your work. It's unlikely that you will be a guest on top-rated talk shows repeating the bold statements in your first book. Most authors have to write at least a few books before they write a bestseller.

This was how I got myself stuck in a major writer's block for a couple weeks: thinking my book was a HUGE deal. When I realized the whole world had better things to do than read or even think about my book, my creative juices flowed freely again.

This is your first book, and I am willing to bet you will write a few more because…

**Writing a book is like getting a tattoo:**
**You always want one more :)**

In 2019, right before the launch of my second book called "Find Your Voice on Social Media", I was at a conference in San Diego. Rachel Hollis got up on stage and shared some very timely and helpful wisdom. First, she told us (don't quote me on this) that she had started out as a food blogger, then wrote cook books and teen fiction. It wasn't until she wrote her sixth book - yes - SIX BOOKS - that she had a bestseller. I decided then and there to write my third book ASAP, followed by three more in the next three years. And that's exactly what I did.

Next, Rachel Hollis said that being scared to post on social media is silly because very few people will actually pay attention to it. This wasn't an issue for me, as I've always felt comfortable sharing my fun times and Aha! moments on social media. However, I began sharing this "nobody cares" tip with my marketing school students (mostly perfectionists and over-thinkers) and it has been extremely helpful for them!

Lastly, she shared this PURE GOLD social media tip:

**No one remembers _what_ you post on social media.**
**They remember that you took the time to show up.**

This was an Aha! moment for me because I was still trying to reverse-engineer my social media success so I could teach it. It made sense that my posts made people feel like I cared about them, even when I wasn't sharing anything profound or useful at that moment. My mission has always been to show people I care by building things they need, asking for feedback, listening to their feedback and showing up consistently as a real human. It has never been about money or recognition for me, although plenty of that has come into my life!

When you make an effort to stay aligned with your servant heart, you know your role. You know that a huge part of your why is to help people live better lives. And when it comes to using social media as a marketing tool, the ones who continue to show up no matter what are not focused on their bank account or how their hair looks or memorizing a script for the video they are about to shoot. They are focused on making sure their niche group of people feel seen, heard and cared for.

## The entrepreneur mindset

Being an entrepreneur means your brain has different wiring than most people's brains. You're a creative genius who must do something impactful with the knowledge in your head, otherwise you feel an annoying pressure like your brain is about to explode. When you have an idea for a blog or video, you can't sleep and your only choice is to get the thoughts out of your head and in Google Docs or your notebook.

When creativity strikes while you're putting your kids to bed, you might as well tuck them in, perhaps grab a coffee and sit down at your laptop to enjoy a few hours of uninterrupted writing time, even though that wasn't your plan. Then take a much deserved nap the next day once the kids are at school. It's not what everyone else around you is doing, but are any of them writing books?

If you want a better life than most you have to do things most aren't willing to do.

Writing a book isn't for everyone. I do feel everyone SHOULD write a book, but I know that most lack the determination and the burning desire I felt as I wrote this, and that you're feeling right now.

In order to succeed as a business owner, we must surround ourselves with other go-getter entrepreneurs. Writing a book is no different. That's why I will remind you again and again to BE VERY CAREFUL WHO YOU ARE SURROUNDING YOURSELF WITH. Choose people who elevate and support you.

## Your five people

Who are the five people you are in contact with the most?

Write their names and a score of 1-5 for each of the following:

| Name | Support and encouragement they give you | Ambition and drive to succeed | Joy and fulfillment in their own lives | Total Score |
|---|---|---|---|---|
| 1. | | | | |
| 2. | | | | |
| 3. | | | | |
| 4. | | | | |
| 5. | | | | |

## Circle your answers:

Do you believe you are the sum of the five people you spend the most time with? **Yes / No**

Do you want to find a new friend or two who would gladly support your book writing session by bringing you Starbucks at 9:00pm? **Yes / No**

Will you take a break from the friends who don't encourage or believe in you until your book is complete? **Yes / No**

# Drinking beer with my friends

You will have days - sometimes a few in a row - when you do NOT feel inspired to write, or when other things seem more worthy of your attention than writing your book.

When people barge into what should be your precious writing time inviting you on exciting adventures, remember this:

Just because it wasn't part of your plan to get distracted from writing your book doesn't mean you can't *enjoy a short distraction* before moving on.

After many days of getting tons of awesome writing done, it's OK to pause the road trip to enjoy the pretty views and fun people in a town you didn't even know existed.

However, after a day or two of enjoying an unexpected and enjoyable break, *get back on the road.*

Beware of giving your future self too much credit for being smarter and more determined than your present self. A short break from writing can make space for fresh ideas and build your writing momentum. It's like an elastic band being stretched until it's released as you sit down at your computer to enjoy a burst of creative energy. But telling yourself day after day "I'll do it tomorrow" gives your future self too much credit.

Procrastination is a bad habit, but it's fixable.

While writing my first book, what slowed my writing momentum many times was drinking beer with my friends. After a few days at my computer, muttering nonsense to my dog, I would miss my friends and want a mini-celebration of what I had accomplished so far. Or sometimes I wouldn't even feel I needed or deserved a break when Friday night would roll around and my friends were wondering if I'd be joining them at so-and-so's house, or at the pub.

The closer I got to 40, the less I had run-aways. Now that I'm over 40, and I know the book writing process inside and out, I know how to enjoy mini-celebrations with fewer beers.

It has taken many years of getting to know myself as a writer. I now know my patterns and the culprits which try to sneak in and sabotage my writing progress. I don't beat myself up, nor am I shocked when I find myself behind schedule, watching Netflix waiting out the *too many beers last night* brain fog. I don't let the Perfectionism Beast convince me all is lost and I should give up. I recognize what happened and wait for my creative juices to start flowing again. And they always do.

Have faith that you will get to know yourself as a writer, and in your ability to get back on track and keep going.

**By the way, I wrote these last few pages while laying on a yoga mat outside sipping a beer.**

I'll wait to enjoy my second beer after this creative surge subsides, and I won't have more than three beers today so that I can keep on my writing schedule!

Now it's time for you to meet another one of the fabulous **FemAuthors** who contributed her wisdom to this book...

A few months after Carey's book was born, I was ready to help more Fempreneurs bring their book ideas to life. I hopped on Instagram Live one evening talking about my new program called "FemAuthors", four months of writing and self-publishing coaching for a small group of women. Noreen Music was watching my Instagram Live video. When I said, *"If you want to write a book, be brave and tell us in the comments!"* she immediately typed,

**"I want to write a book!"**

## Tips for Becoming An Author from Noreen Music

Noreen, how did it feel to complete your book?

*There's nothing quite like the feeling of staring at a blank page, knowing that you have the power to fill it with your knowledge and talent to benefit others. For me, this moment was both exhilarating and daunting, as I grappled with the infinite possibilities before me.*

*But as the words started to flow, so too did the thrill of creation. My ideas took shape, my passion poured out onto the page, and my book unfolded in ways I never imagined. It's a rush of creativity that is both intoxicating and overwhelming, as I captured the essence of my vision and my purpose on the blank pages.*

### How did you celebrate the completion of your book?

*The feeling of holding my published book in my hands was indescribable. It was a culmination of months of hard work, dedication, and passion that finally came to fruition. The sense of accomplishment and pride that came with sharing my story and skills with the world was unmatched. I poured all of myself into my book, and seeing it in print was a validation of my dedication, sacrifice and hard work.*

*But the celebration didn't end there. My writing partner (Felicia Yap, Reel Awesome Productions) along with Lyndsie Barrie and myself decided to create a book launch event that included a workshop for fempreneurs followed by a celebration with our family and friends. That event is when I really knew my words would continue to touch people's lives for years to come. What a powerful feeling. And even if my book never becomes a "bestseller", the fact that it exists in the world is something I'm very proud of. I created something that will outlast me, and that is a truly remarkable achievement.*

### How has becoming an Author helped your career?

*As a fempreneur, you are constantly seeking ways to stand out from the competition. Writing a book is one of the most effective ways to do just that. In fact, according to a survey by Forbes, 96% of business owners believe that writing a book gives them a competitive edge. This has certainly been my experience.*

*I've met some incredible people along my writing journey because the book opened the door to personal and professional connections. When I give a copy of my book to a prospective client, they get to know me in ways that I simply can't replace any other way. Even my website doesn't forge the same kind of connection and understanding that my book, and the heart and soul written on the pages, does.*

*Not only can writing a book help you establish credibility and increase your revenue, but it can also open up new opportunities and relationships for you. It has the power to take your entrepreneurial career to the next level.*

## How is your personal life different now that you're an Author?

*Writing a book can be a transformative experience, not just for your career but also for your personal life. In my case, writing my book had a profound impact on my relationships with family and friends.*

*During the process of writing my book, I found myself delving into personal experiences and memories that I had not shared with my family before. As I wrote about these experiences, I felt a sense of catharsis and healing that allowed me to open up more to my loved ones. I also found that my family members were more interested in my writing and my creative process than I had anticipated. They became my biggest cheerleaders and supporters, which brought us closer together.*

*Writing a book is a time-consuming and solitary process, which can make it difficult to maintain social connections. However, I found that my friends were more understanding and supportive than I had expected. They respected my need for alone time and were eager to hear about my progress. I also found that my writing gave us new topics to discuss and explore, which brought a fresh energy to our conversations. Overall, I felt that my friendships grew deeper and more meaningful as a result of my writing.*

*As the saying goes, 'The pen is mightier than the sword.' And for fempreneurs, this couldn't be more true. By putting your thoughts and ideas into words, you have the power to inspire, educate, and motivate others. So why not take advantage of this powerful tool? Start writing today and see where it takes you.*

## Noreen's Top 5 Tips for Completing a Book:

1. *Work with a writing coach for brainstorming, accountability and help to push through when it gets hard. Choose someone who has completed at least one book so you can lean on them at all stages of your writing journey.*

2. *Have faith that you can do it. It may seem daunting at first, but if you choose positive thoughts and self-talk, you will do it! Imagine yourself holding your books in your hands and what it will feel like. Or even better, handing a copy to each of your new clients!*

3. *Be really clear on "WHY" you're writing a book. Write down your top 5 reasons why you won't quit and post it where you can see it. This is your anchor when you want to quit or you have doubts about your ability.*

4. *Create a framework for your book before you start writing so you feel less scattered. Knowing the topics you want to write about helps break down the process into small, manageable chunks.*

5. *Let your book title reveal itself to you even if it's near the end of the writing process. The title is not the most critical part of this journey. Creating the wire-frame and the writing is.*

## Lastly, what was one of the most difficult parts of writing a book?

*The struggle is real. While writing a book is an incredibly rewarding experience, it also takes a significant emotional toll. The process of pouring my heart and soul into a project at times left me feeling drained, anxious, and overwhelmed.*

*To navigate the emotional toll of writing a book, I made sure to prioritize self-care. This included taking breaks when I needed them, seeking support from my writing partner, coaches and loved ones, and I made sure to continue engaging in activities that brought me joy and relaxation.*

*It's also important to set realistic expectations. Recognize that writing a book is a marathon, not a sprint. It's okay to take your time and make mistakes along the way.*

It's Lyndsie here again. Now that you're all-in, it is important to know what it will feel like if you change your mind. Write your answers:

**Describe what it would feel like if you decided to quit writing this book for any reason:**

WRITE YOUR DAMN BOOK, WOMAN! BY LYNDSIE BARRIE

**What opportunities will you miss out on if you decide not to become an Author?**

# Chapter 3:

# Before we hit the road, let's look at the map

Noreen highlighted two of the most important steps on the roadmap to becoming an Author:

- Write the 5 reasons why you won't quit

- Create your book framework

When something throws you off course, these are the best 2 tools to have on hand for getting back on track. You will complete these two writing assignments soon.

## You deserve success

My prediction is the first thing that will throw you off course will be a lack of boundaries. When someone doesn't feel they deserve success, or they are afraid of success for any reason, their boundaries are weak or non-existent. They sabotage their success without realizing it.

Examples of **weak boundaries** include not staying focused during your writing timeblock, or putting it off until later in the day when your mind isn't as sharp.

People with no boundaries at all keep pushing their marketing and writing timeblocks to tomorrow. They allow less important tasks to trump what is required to meet their writing and marketing goals.

The roadmap I'm about to show you includes instructions for creating boundaries because without boundaries you won't get far on this writing road trip. For example, your closest friends and family need to know you will not jump out of the moving vehicle at their request. You will say no to a few, but not all, parties and events if they interfere with your writing or marketing timeblocks.

But like Noreen said, it's okay to take your time and make mistakes along the way. You will miss a turn or end up on the side of the road with a flat tire once or twice. Each time, you will use the steps and checklists herein to get back on the road.

**The roadmap** shows you how to keep moving forward from milestone to milestone; it's the **schedule** for completing your book in four months or less. Each milestone will take 1-2 weeks to complete. There are 12 milestones.

**The weekly marketing checklist** holds you accountable to continuing to write your book by taking your social media followers and fans behind-the-scenes into your **#authorlife**.

As you read through the milestones and marketing steps, don't panic if you aren't sure how to do something. The remaining chapters will walk you through how to complete these tasks. Plus there are videos showing you how to do the "techy" things at yycfempreneurs.com/author.

Simply read through the milestones for now. Later you will come back and write a deadline date on the line below each milestone.

# MILESTONE 1

☐ Announce on social media that you are writing a book!

☐ Book and complete a professional photo shoot. Gently nudge your photographer to send you at least one awesome shot while they're editing the images.

☐ Set up a Google Drive Folder for all your writing at drive.google.com. Add a new Google Docs in the folder.

☐ Write your "Nine Stories" in Google Docs.

*Deadline:*
_____

# MILESTONE 2

☐ Write your "Essential Topics" in Google Docs.

☐ Build your "Book Framework" - write it in your notebook.

☐ Write "My 5 Reasons Why" in Google Docs. *(The 5 reasons why you will complete this book.)*

☐ Publish your first "Book Sneak Peek" blog post, or put it on Facebook or LinkedIn if you don't have a website.

*Deadline:* _____

WRITE YOUR DAMN BOOK, WOMAN! BY LYNDSIE BARRIE

# MILESTONE 3

☐ Write your "Book Purpose Sentence".

☐ Build a survey at mailchimp.com.

☐ Set up your "Upcoming Book" lead magnet at mailchimp.com.

***The "techy" steps are all explained and demonstrated in free videos at yycfempreneurs.com/author.
Don't worry! I've got you!

Deadline:
_____

# MILESTONE 4

☐ Add a FREE GIFT button to your website home page, if you have a website (button links to survey).

☐ Add the survey link to your Instagram bio.

☐ Post an image that says, "May I have your opinion?" with a teaser from your book and survey link on Facebook and/or LinkedIn.

☐ If you haven't yet this week, tease about your latest blog on your top 2 social channels with one of your professional images. Caption starts with: "New Blog Post Alert!"

WRITE YOUR DAMN BOOK, WOMAN!   BY LYNDSIE BARRIE

# MILESTONE 4 CONTINUED

☐ **Review your survey data to see what respondents want included in your book.**

☐ **Create a Goal Board Version of your Book Framework. Put it up on a wall in your house where others will see it and add to your accountability.**

Deadline:

_____

# MILESTONE 5

☐ With your cell phone, shoot 3 "Quick Win" videos about 3 of your Essential Topics. Keep the videos in your phone so they're ready to post according to your Weekly Marketing Checklist.

☐ Publish on YouTube one of your 3 "Quick Win" videos 3 days in a row.

☐ Learn how and why to use hashtags and build your hashtag bank using the free guide at yycfempreneurs.com/hashtags. Begin adding 10-30 hashtags to every social media post using your hashtag bank.

☐ At mailchimp.com, email a brand new piece of writing to your new subscribers. Follow the instructions at yycfempreneurs.com/author to complete this step.

Deadline: _____

WRITE YOUR DAMN BOOK, WOMAN!  BY LYNDSIE BARRIE

# MILESTONE 6

☐ Invite 6-10 editors to read and provide feedback on your book. You will also ask your editors to choose their favorite from a list of 3-4 title ideas. Follow the "Editor Invite" steps in chapter 6.

☐ Continue sending out the "Editor Invite" until you have a minimum of 4 people who are currently editing the first 2-3 chapters of your book.

☐ Write down the names of any Authors you know who would be willing to skim (or fully read) your manuscript and provide you with a testimonial for the first page of your book.

Deadline:

WRITE YOUR DAMN BOOK, WOMAN!   BY LYNDSIE BARRIE

# MILESTONE 7

☐ Read the suggestions made by your editors. Update your Essential Topics and Book Framework according to the feedback you have received.

☐ Send the next 2-3 chapters to your editors. Include your 3-4 book title ideas and ask your editors to pick their favourite. Also ask for their book title ideas.

☐ Walk through a bookstore to decide what style of book cover you want. Notice colours, fonts and placement of images. Take pictures with your cell phone of your favorites. Ask yourself: *do I want my photo on the front cover?*

☐ Think ahead to your book launch party: *will you want to give away bookmarks or pens with your website on them? Will you want a photographer?* If so, make the necessary arrangements now.

*Deadline:*
_____

# MILESTONE 8

☐ Send the last chapters to your editors - one week deadline.

☐ Read the suggestions made by your editors and which book title they like best. Update your Essential Topics and Book Framework according to the feedback you have received.

☐ Create 3 draft book covers, each with a different title, at canva.com. Use the cover templates and instructions at yycfempreneurs.com/author.

☐ Create a "Book Cover Vote" image at canva.com with text: "Book Cover A, B or C?" In the caption ask people to vote in the comments and state when the vote will end (in 7 days).

# MILESTONE 8 CONTINUED

☐ Boost on Instagram and/or Facebook: "Book Cover Vote" image: $5-10/day for 7 days.

☐ Share the "Book Cover Vote" post to your Instagram/Facebook story every other day. Each time, let people know how many more days are left to vote.

☐ Read and respond to every comment below your "Book Cover Vote" post with: *"Thanks for voting! May I ask for one more quick favour? Which title do you think is best?"*

☐ On the last day of your book cover vote, share the post on your Instagram story with text across: "LAST DAY TO VOTE!"

Deadline: _____

WRITE YOUR DAMN BOOK, WOMAN!  BY LYNDSIE BARRIE

# MILESTONE 9

☐ Read the suggestions made by your editors.

☐ Update your Essential Topics and Book Framework according to the feedback you have received.

☐ Begin formatting your book. Follow the instructions in the video at yycfempreneurs.com/author.

☐ Finalize your book cover. You can unveil it this week on social media and your website with "COMING SOON" across the image, or wait to use it next week for marketing your book launch party.

☐ Secure a location for your book launch party and set up your ticket link. Your book launch party should be 3-4 weeks away because it is the last step in Milestone 12.

Deadline: _____

# MILESTONE 10

☐ Write your back cover description. Then copy and paste it into your Amazon book description in the next step...

☐ Upload your book to kdp.amazon.com. Once it's approved (usually within 48 hours), order 3 copies. Do not order "Author Copies" because they take FOREVER. These first 3 copies are for you and 2 editors to look for layout, spelling or grammar issues and mark them with a red pen.

☐ When your books arrive, make a video of you opening the envelope and holding up your 3 book babies - BE EXCITED!! YOU DID IT!! But do not post these images yet because *you want to fix any errors before people start ordering your book.* Drop off copies with two local editors and give them 48 hours to read it and mark any errors with a red pen.

☐ Read your copy with a red pen, marking any errors you find.

WRITE YOUR DAMN BOOK, WOMAN! BY LYNDSIE BARRIE

# MILESTONE 10 CONTINUED

☐ Once you have all 3 "red pen" copies in your hands, sit down at your computer, open your book manuscript (the KDP template, not in Google Docs) and fix the errors.

☐ Upload the updated template (in the same book) at kdp.amazon.com.

☐ As soon as you see the email saying your book is live, order 3 more copies and post the picture of you holding your book babies on all your social channels with the book launch party link.

☐ Talk about your book launch party on social media every other day. Make sure to add the link to buy tickets to your Instagram stories.

Deadline: _____

# MILESTONE 11

☐ Spread the word about your book launch party in as many ways as you can think of. There's no right or wrong way - just have fun with it! Get your friends and book editors involved by asking,

*"Can you think of a fun way to build more awareness about my upcoming book?"*

☐ Print and distribute/post on bulletin boards book launch flyers with a QR code for either/both:

- book launch party tickets
- buy on Amazon

☐ Continue to increase your social media momentum this week and next week by boosting your book launch party image on Instagram and/or Facebook. This investment will have a huge impact on your life and business!

Deadline: _____

# MILESTONE 12

☐ Read the BONUS "Party Planning" chapter at the end of this book. Make sure you have done everything you want to do to prepare for your book launch party.

☐ CELEBRATE! YOU DID IT, WOMAN!!!

Deadline: _____

# WEEKLY MARKETING CHECKLIST

*Begin using this checklist after you've completed Milestone 1.

*Cycle through the following 8 posts on the same 2 channels.

**Your goal is to post 5x/week.**

- [ ] Head outside and shoot a video sharing a few of the reasons why you're excited to be writing this book, or what you're loving most about the writing process. Or you could talk about the new blog post and direct people to your website to read it.

- [ ] Show your audience something you like to do for fun in a selfie or timelapse/hyperlapse video.

- [ ] Offer your FREE GIFT - a draft chapter of your upcoming book - in exchange for their opinion. Give them clear instructions:

  *Go to my website and click the **FREE GIFT** button!*

- [ ] Post a writing selfie: a behind the scenes glimpse of you in #writingmode with a taste of what you're writing in the caption. Mix up the camera angle and/or location each time - have fun with it!

# WEEKLY MARKETING CHECKLIST
### *continued*

☐ Interview a complimentary business owner on Instagram Live, YouTube Live, or Facebook Live.

☐ Shout out a local small business or promote your upcoming Instagram Live with a local business owner.

☐ Publish a new blog post: a new sneak peek of what you've been writing. In the middle and at the end of your blog post add, *"May I please have your opinion? I'd be so grateful to have your feedback on this draft chapter and learn what you'd like to read about in my upcoming book. Here is the link: (survey link). Thank you!"*

☐ Add text across one of your new professional photos: "New Blog Post Alert!" The caption is the first 2-3 paragraphs from your new blog post followed by, *"Read more at (your website)."*

Use the "Video Marketing Checklist" in chapter 4

if you need help with shooting and posting videos.

You can print the milestones and checklists at
yycfempreneurs.com/author.

## Take a deep breath

Do you feel a little overwhelmed, like I just asked you to
drive across all 52 states in one day?

Now that you have the schedule, checklists and instructional
videos ready, we're going to slow down to real-life speed and
*get to work.*

*If this is your first time reading this book, read it to the end,
then **get to work.***

WRITE YOUR DAMN BOOK, WOMAN!  BY LYNDSIE BARRIE

# Chapter 4:

## Get in the PURPLE zone

Creativity takes time, which is why you need to block your calendar for a minimum of 2 hours at a time to write. And like Carey said, it took her at least 30 minutes to get sorted, log on, find where she wanted to start and get in the flow at the beginning of each writing timeblock. You might need to book 4 hour blocks like Carey did. And definitely make your writing blocks PURPLE in your calendar like Carey did!

Unfortunately adding purple writing timeblocks to our calendar doesn't guarantee we will be blessed with infinite wisdom and energy. We can't control when we get into our "creative zone", or where. Trust me, I've tried. We can, however, find places and times of the day when we tend to be more creative.

**Creativity comes to those who put out the welcome mat, open the door and make an effort to be present.**

The satisfaction from creating something awesome feels AMAZING for everyone - artists and athletes alike. The "creative zone" looks different for each of us, but we can all agree there's nothing like being "in the zone".

When I am on a mission to write a book I set aside 2-5 hours a day three to four days a week in the mornings. This has changed since writing my first book when my son was young and I was making him breakfast and driving him to school. Back then I wrote mostly in the evenings after putting him to bed. I would write until 2:00 - 3:00am, sleep until 7:00am, take him to school, check email and take care of my financial business, take a nap, walk the dog, pick him up from school, and repeat.

Now that my son is in high school and drives himself everywhere it's doable to structure my life around writing in the mornings. I find my brain is fresh and clear in the mornings, however I do not write every day. I aim to write every other day so that on my non-writing days I can get caught up on other work.

## Why don't more women give themselves the gift of <u>time</u> to be creative?

Most of the women I've worked with are mothers who feel their number one job is to take care of their children. We moms often feel it is selfish to set aside time to be creative, even though the way we show up as mothers hugely improves once boundaries are in place around creative time!

When more women allow themselves time to create, more women will bring their book ideas to life. This is one of the many reasons why it's so important for you to <u>document your writing journey on social media:</u> ***you will inspire more women to create books and businesses!***

**What will stop you from posting selfies and videos of your writing journey on social media?**

☐ Imagine yourself shooting and posting a video on Instagram right now and then write down any objections or concerns that come to mind.

☐ Why do so many women have trouble using social media to its full life-changing potential? What's holding them back? Write your ideas.

Check the boxes after recording your thoughts in your notebook.

After working with hundreds of Fempreneurs I've found the culprit is a complex and hairy-seeming beast...

# Perfectionism

Good News: You created the Perfectionism Beast, so you can un-create it.

The beast tried messing with me when I was 28 years old. I had accepted a job offer which required me to learn and do tons of new things: take courses, pass exams, wear blazers and speak with confidence to people about the most private subject in their lives...

**MONEY.**

You can imagine what the beast had to say:

*Imposter! You know nothing about managing money! No one will trust your financial advice!*

I didn't back down because I had nothing to lose and so much to gain if I pulled it off.

My dad's reaction was so cute when I told him I was training to be a "Financial Advisor".

*"You've got balls to do that",* he said. He was shocked, which I loved.

The beast didn't get far with me, and I believe I have my parents to thank for this. They weren't big risk takers themselves. They both had government jobs because of the pension. But they rewarded their children with VERY LOUD PRAISE when we were brave.

For me, it was singing and playing the piano that built my confidence. I was far from comfortable with singing and playing piano in public, but I liked when it was over and I felt proud. I knew I had done something most people were too afraid to do. And I liked my parents and music teachers praising me.

One time my dad actually told me he wasn't happy with my plan. I was 18 and wanted to go to hairdressing school. He was not a fan of this. But when I started my own mobile beauty company, which I ran for eight years, he changed his tune. Especially because I was able to support myself and my son as a single mom. Hairdressing was, and is, an extremely flexible and awesome career for young women. My dad eventually said he was glad I decided to become a hairdresser.

A series of very serendipitous events led me to being one of 20+ new hires at a large international investment firm. I was the only trainee who was switching from "Hair Stylist" to "Money Stylist". It was the fact that I had been self-employed for 8 years which landed me the job. They said being self-motivated and knowing how to talk to people were necessary skills and they would teach me the rest. But first, I had to pass a few exams, including the Canadian Securities Course and Life Licence Qualification Program. As I completed difficult courses and training, my Saskatchewan-born dad continued to call me "ballsy". I loved it.

Many people work their way up from being "average", by North American standards, to having huge success and credibility. I knew it was possible for myself to do this, which is what gave me the "balls" to dismiss the beast's lies. Instead of focusing on and giving power to the negative thoughts, I focused on the "rags to riches" stories I had heard. I read books and listened to podcasts that fueled my fire. I chose to become someone who does and says things most people don't do and say. I stuck to the bumpy road, full of mistakes and embarrassing moments, trusting it would get smoother and eventually lead to the success I wanted. I took away the beast's power by taking action, even when it was uncomfortable, or when I had doubts.

## The *Fake It Til You Make It* phase

I knew it was time to quit faking it when my heart told me to be myself. I began embracing my small town roots and quickly found that most of my clients were also from small towns. They liked that about me. I talked about my love for the outdoors, hunting and camping. My best clients, many of which are still my clients today, liked the real me. In the beginning I was often tempted to pretend to be someone I'm not because I worried the "small town girl" wasn't what they wanted in a Financial Advisor. It was the beast telling me a lie - that the real me wasn't good enough. I chose to trust my heart instead of the beast and the more I did that, the more ideal clients I found.

After three years at the investment firm they let me go because I wasn't bringing in enough commissions. It was devastating, yet such a blessing in disguise. I hadn't been able to serve people the way I was meant to. The commission targets and constraints on my social media content were crushing my creativity and joy.

As soon as I set myself up as an Independent Financial Consultant, I donated all but one of my blazers to a thrift store and began experimenting with shooting videos and posting them on YouTube. Then I hired a business coach who helped me write a book. And while I was writing my book, I tried all sorts of marketing things, some of which were very successful.

## *"How do I market my book while I write it?"*

This is where your **Nine Stories** come into play. These babies are going to be your most valuable social media content, even though some of them might not end up in your book.

As you write each of your Nine Stories, think about how you have become the person you are today. If you think your stories about mentors, pinch-me moments and accomplishments are not unique or exciting, it's a lie. And you know where it's coming from.

*The best social media system I've found is posting a mix of your personal stories and tips/tricks which are specifically for your niche audience.*

Aside from what to post, the next question is, *"Which social channels should I be posting on?"*

Your answer: choose 2 channels to post on 4-5 times each week.

Because you're writing and marketing <u>your first book</u>, a once in a lifetime experience and marketing opportunity, you want to post at least 5x/week on your 2 channels.

***Write the 2 social media channels you will post on consistently:***

I ***LOVE*** writing books because it is another way to do what I love most of all:

MARKETING.

What I love most about helping a Fempreneur become an Author is the thousands of JUICY social media posts she gains. Her book is filled with valuable and empowering information that can be easily repurposed into social media posts. And this makes me SO HAPPY because I know that she will <u>never again</u> feel social media stuck!

Even though the "Perfectionism Beast" never really bothered me, my Fempreneur Marketing School students showed me the damage it can do. The beast actually stops women in their tracks and leaves them feeling helpless and frustrated.

Once you stare perfectionism in the face and really see it for what it is - pure illusion - you can choose to turn this beast into something else. You can rewire your brain to label "fear" as "excitement" instead. You have the power to react in a positive way to the exact same feeling.

**Here are the common lies perfectionism says to writers who are marketing their book on social media:**

*- Everyone who sees your face on social media thinks you are an imposter.*

*- You are going to mess up and embarrass yourself on social media. And then all your friends will judge you.*

*- You aren't pretty enough to have your face on social media, or on the cover of a book. And your hair looks stupid.*

*- Someone has already written the book you're trying to write and they did a better job than you will.*


**Ouch, right??!!**

The beast's awful lies come from people in our lives who have said mean words to us. Or it could be someone who never said anything - kind, mean, or otherwise - but their facial expression or dismissive reaction left us with negative thoughts and what ifs.

I wish we were sitting together right now so I could compliment the heck out of you, and then have you repeat my compliments aloud and REALLY OWN THEM. If I were there with beautiful, unique you right now, together we would shrink the beast's power.

But since I am not with you, let's instead think about someone in your life who always supports you and believes in you more than you believe in yourself. Write their name on the next page.


This is an optional writing exercise, in case you need it:

## Write the name of your #1 supporter:

Each time a negative thought comes, clearly identify where it's coming from: the beast or your #1 supporter (the name you wrote above.) Draw a line down the center of a blank page in your notebook. Make 2 lists:

| The Beast | Name (your #1 supporter) |
| --- | --- |
| | |

Each time the beast tells you something negative, write it down. Immediately write the message your #1 supporter has for you that counteracts what the beast said.

Another way of looking at this, if you can't think of a mentor or friend who always cheers you on, is think about **what your five year old self would say to the beast.** Does that little girl want you to take risks and step out of your comfort zone? Does she look up to you and believe you can do anything?

Five year old you believes there's more abundance, joy and fulfillment in your future if you continue putting one foot in front of the other. Five year old you doesn't carry the baggage of other people's projections. She's free and excited to live a full life, and *she knows who you really are.*

When the beast tells you it's normal to feel stuck and unfulfilled, or that you aren't good enough, write it down. Then write the true messages from your #1 supporter and/or your five year old self.

Perhaps give your "Perfectionism Beast" a hideous name. Maybe it's your mean step mother or physics teacher - someone who didn't encourage you and left you feeling unloved or insecure. When you hear the lies, call them out and switch your focus to the messages from those who believe you can do anything.

If this book results in you experiencing one improvement in your life, I want it to be that you **STOP LISTENING TO THE PERFECTIONISM BEAST**

And to be frank, your book will not come to life in the shadow of perfectionism. It needs the sunshine that is your creativity to blossom.


## Vroom Vroom

Grab your suitcase and road trip snacks, get in the truck **(there's a photo of your sexy, reliable 4x4 ride on the next page)**, buckle up your seatbelt, and crank the tunes.

It's time to hit the road.

Can you think of any legit reasons for not hopping in this sexy truck and hitting the road today? If so, write them in the left hand column below. On the right, write what you can do to remove this road block and when you will have it done so you can START WRITING YOUR DAMN BOOK, WOMAN!

| Reasons why I can't start writing my book today: | What I'll do to remove this roadblock and when it will be done: |
|---|---|
|  |  |

If you want to wait to start writing your book until you feel smarter, prettier or less busy, that's procrastination talking. And you know where that came from - not your #1 supporter or your five year old self. No matter what you may feel is blocking the road, know this:

The best way to take away some of the beast's power is to TAKE ACTION.

If you are not ready to start today for a legitimate reason, decide when you will start and ask a few people to hold you accountable to starting when you say you will. They will know when you actually start writing your book because this is your first step in Milestone 1...

Announce on social media that you are writing a book. The most engaging and interesting way to do this is **in a video!**

Right now you have 2 choices: start writing your book today, or wait until you think you will be more ready. If you are leaning towards the second option, don't stop reading this book. Read this entire book and then complete Milestone 1 when you have removed the roadblocks (or when you're feeling more brave.)

**Warning:** humans give their future selves too much credit. We all do it. We believe we will be more dedicated, focused, ready - WHATEVER - next week or next month. And it's rarely true.

There is no better time than now.

If you need a few days or a week to schedule time to write every week, that's fine. But if you're thinking you'll be more ready to start a month or more from now, here's what you need to do:

## Less overthinking and more taking action!

My superpower is helping perfectionistic Fempreneurs over-think less and take action more.

What does "overthinking" look like for you? What is stopping you from posting a video <u>right now</u> saying that TODAY you have begun writing a book?

These 2 things would stop most women from posting the video:

- comparing herself to others and feeling inadequate

- worrying about what others might think of her

Did you know these things are actually not real? They are simply thoughts, and they were <u>not</u> dreamed up by your wise inner self.

Choosing to focus on ANY negative thought gives it power. Choosing to do ONE THING that moves you towards the book writing finish line empowers your TRUE LIMITLESS SELF!

It's your choice.

Rather than letting worst-case scenarios play out in your mind, take action. Grab your phone right now, head outside and record a video of you announcing that you are writing a book. It doesn't matter if you've actually written even one sentence of your book. Announcing your upcoming book on social media will provide the fuel to move forward. The "fuel" I'm referring to is ACCOUNTABILITY.

Use the checklist on the next page to shoot a short video ASAP sharing who your book is for and how it will help them.

Use this wording to announce in your video that you're writing a book:

*"Hello everyone! I am super nervous right now, but I have a really important announcement so I'm stepping out of my comfort zone to make this video... My announcement is: I am writing a book! I don't know what it will be called yet, but it is a book for (who it is for) to help them (the problem it will solve). I will have more details for you soon! Stay tuned and thanks for your encouragement and support as I bring my book to life!"*

# VIDEO CREATION CHECKLIST

Follow these steps to shoot and post quick and simple videos on social media:

- ☐ Shoot outside whenever possible. Outdoor videos get more views.

- ☐ Wear a bright coloured shirt, hat or pair of glasses.

- ☐ Do not wear sunglasses - your eyes are the window to your soul.

- ☐ Pretend there is only one person watching - your most encouraging and easy-going friend or family member.

- ☐ Hold your phone straight out from your face at eye-level (no selfie stick or gadgets required).

- ☐ <u>Most important: SMILE! Be excited!!</u>

- ☐ Record using your phone's camera app. Do not record in the Instagram app, or the TikTok app, or other social media app. This is so you have the videos stored in your phone gallery for future use.

After posting your book announcement video on at least two social channels, check all the boxes for Milestone 1 and CONTINUE READING THIS BOOK.

I want to make sure this is crystal clear: helpful tips and stories for completing Milestone 1 are coming up in this chapter.

## Do this now:

☐ Flip back and write your deadline dates at the bottom of all 12 Milestones in Chapter 3. Or print all 12 milestones at yycfempreneurs.com/author and put each page on your goal board with a deadline date, one by one until you've completed all of the milestones.

## Do this every week:

☐ Complete all the steps on the Marketing and Writing Checklists.

It's time for some inspiration from another FemAuthor.

The night I hopped on Instagram Live to share my new FemAuthors program, Noreen wasn't the only woman watching who wanted to write a book…

## Tips for Becoming An Author from Felicia Yap

Felicia, how did it feel to complete your book?

*Imagine what it feels like to be pregnant. As you grow a baby inside you, you'll experience magical moments and challenging ones. When the baby's ready to enter the world, you'll probably feel nervous and excited. That's how I felt. I was scared about what people would think about me and my book because I shared vulnerable stories and experiences between its covers. But I knew my book would help those who read it so I pushed hard to the finish line. Holding the physical copy of my book, "Don't Stay a Secret" for the first time was like holding my baby. It made my heart sing!*

*I spent hundreds of hours working on my book to make it valuable and enjoyable to read. All that time spent working on my book meant time away from my two young daughters and my husband. I was so glad that I could be more present with them once it was finished. I completed the book while I was pregnant with my third child. Since the book was published before my son was born, I joke that the book is my third baby.*

## How did you celebrate the completion of your book?

My book-writing partner, Noreen Music and I planned a special event to inspire and celebrate women entrepreneurs alongside the release of our books. In the afternoon, we interviewed several female business owners, who shared all sorts of valuable stories and tips. In the evening, our friends and family joined us to celebrate with speeches, dinner and a cake with images of both our books on it. It was an event I will never forget.

## Tell us a story about one of the best connections you made because of your book.

*One of the best connections I've made through writing my book has been meeting Lyndsie Barrie. Writing a book hadn't crossed my mind until Lyndsie suggested that I write one. I ditched the doubt and decided to go for it. Lyndsie was a great cheerleader as I went through the book-writing journey. Being a part of her Fempreneur community has made being a solopreneur less lonely.*

## How is your business different now that you're an Author?

*Although I have more than 20 years of experience as a video storyteller, I faced a lot of imposter syndrome and lacked confidence when it came to pricing my services. I now have physical proof that I am an expert in my field of video storytelling - I literally wrote the book on it!*

*Even if someone can't work with me in person, they can read my stories and learn practical tips that I've gained as a TV news anchor, digital content creator and videographer. The knowledge and experience that I share in the book is worth thousands of dollars. I wish I had a book like mine when I was starting to create videos. I've also released the audiobook version of my book which I voiced and I am so proud of it!*

*People in different parts of the country have chosen me as their Video Confidence Coach because I'm one of the few in my industry who have written a book. Seeing my book gives them confidence that I know what I'm talking about and that I can help them. And my book is a valuable tool in my business to help my students learn faster and retain the information.*

*I love public speaking and being an Author has provided me with more speaking opportunities. I've been hired as a paid speaker at a women's business event because the organizer found my book on Amazon and read it. I was also asked to speak at a different women's conference where I got to share my story, talk about my book, and connect with other female entrepreneurs.*

## How is your personal life different now that you're an Author?

*My husband was inspired by my book writing journey and decided to write a book to help parents yell less and connect more with their kids. It's called "Big-Hearted Parenting: Even When it Seems Impossible". He says he didn't know it was possible for someone who wasn't an avid writer to finish a book. Now we have two Authors in our family. I'm so proud of what he's accomplished and all the families he's helping with his knowledge and his goal to help keep families together.*

## Felicia's Top 5 Tips for completing a book:

1. *Raising a family while writing a book is tough. Ask for help and support. I asked my family to help watch my little girls while I wrote during the day. I wouldn't have been able to finish the book without their support.*

2. *Give yourself a deadline to finish your book and do your best to stick to it. Done is better than perfect. If you're a perfectionist like me, you may feel the urge to keep editing and rewriting your book. At some point, let it go and let others read your book.*

3. *Hire a book writing coach and find someone who is also writing a book to work with. These investments of money and time were very valuable.*

4. *Write. Write. And write some more. Sometimes you'll think of something brilliant to say. Other times, you'll sit in front of a blank screen for a while. When inspiration strikes, have a place – either digital or a notebook –*

*where you can jot down your ideas. Keep writing and your book will take shape over time.*

5. *Start sharing your book-writing journey early on. Share your goal to finish a book with friends and family and on social media. Drum up interest as soon as you start writing to market your book and build an audience.*

<u>Lastly, what was one of the most difficult parts of writing a book?</u>

*One of the hardest parts of writing a book was coming up with the title. I went through so many titles for my book. It was frustrating. In the end I asked my community on Instagram and Facebook to vote for their favourite title out of my top two picks. "Don't Stay a Secret" was the winner.*

*One more thing: Feeling scared about publishing your work is normal. Finish it anyways. It's worth it.*

It's Lyndsie here again. Let's continue crushing Milestone 1.

It's time to make a financial investment in strengthening your online presence and positioning yourself as an authority in your field:

**Book and complete a professional photo shoot. Gently nudge your photographer to send you at least one awesome shot while they're editing the images.**

The goal of this photo shoot is to have 10-20 professional photos to use on social media. You want a few of you working in your business, a few rest & relaxation shots, and a few headshots for the cover of your book.

Ask around for photographer suggestions if you don't have one in mind. If you're not sure what to do with your hair and make up, ask the photographer for guidance.

Soon you will start posting a mix of "real and raw" selfies and professional images on social media.

## The power of your "Nine Stories"

I started writing my second book on my 37th birthday in August, 2019. I rented a little rustic cabin as my own private writing retreat near Salmon Arm, BC. As I sat in front of my computer, watching rain drip off the roof, I thought back to where I was two years ago. I knew exactly where I was and how I felt thanks to Facebook showing me this photo from 2 years ago:

I snapped this *ussie* (a selfie is by yourself) of my son and I on my 35th birthday in a hotel room in Vernon, BC.

The summer I turned 35 was the first summer I had taken completely off of work. I had just written my first book, Money & The 39 Forever Mom, and my financial consulting business was three and a half years old. I felt I had come to a point in my life where I had earned a "selfish summer", or at least that was what I started out believing. By the end of it, I realized my summer hadn't been selfish at all. Sharing what I was up to and getting more real and raw on social media ever before had a huge impact on my community - my clients, friends and family.

*The marketing magic was a result of sharing my stories, both stories from the past and what I was up to during my Selfish Summer.*

People were used to me sharing highlights of my outdoorsy life, but I wasn't ready to be totally real until all of a sudden I felt comfortable with sharing more of my life on social media. My favourite podcasts taught me how to step back, look at everything - all the wins, blessings, challenges I overcame - and be proud and grateful.

Before, I was always chasing, forgetting to look down at how far I had climbed up Success Mountain.

Instead of continuing to look up at where I still had to go, I decided it was time to celebrate the years of persevering. By age 35 I had done a great job of positioning myself as an expert in my field. I was done with worrying about my clients thinking I was a slacker because I posted photos of my fun life too often.

My selfish summer was all about having fun in beautiful places, which meant I had original and eye-catching content daily: camping, horseback riding, eating ice cream and sea kayaking.

Although I didn't realize it until many months later, I was killing it at "online marketing". Opening up about my life created a ripple effect.

Here's what I mean by being "opening up" on social media:

1. Share what you love, what matters most to you, or simply your favourite things to do and why.

2. Explain why you are grateful - for your amazing clients who believe in you enough to choose to work with you, for your health, for the beauty of the earth, for your wonderful family.

3. Share stories about when life was harder for you and you were still figuring things out. Celebrate the struggles you faced that led to your purpose.

4. Document your life. Share what you're up to right now. Take lots of selfies!

I'm sure you've seen social media posts of people opening up about their unfortunate life events. Being "vulnerable" is all the rage these days, but there are different ways to be vulnerable. The way I'm encouraging you to be vulnerable does not include sharing sad stories, or crying, or venting publicly. That's not how entrepreneurs should show up on social media. "Opening up" on social media is all about gratitude for entrepreneurs.

# Marketing Magic: Gratitude

Share real stories from your life and include why you're grateful for the lesson you learned from it. This clearly communicates to your ideal clients:

"THIS IS ALL ABOUT YOU."

Being GRATEFUL for the challenges you've overcome that led you to 10 days in Mexico swimming in the ocean doesn't seem like "bragging". Instead, you are sharing tips and tricks for never quitting, for working hard, for staying committed to serving the right people. That's why you're on the beach in Mexico, and that's why you're posting a selfie with the ocean behind you: to show your existing clients and anyone who has supported you that you're grateful for them.

Are you starting to see how **gratitude** is **marketing magic**?

Here's an example of something I shared on social media during my "selfish summer":

My son and I were on the ferry heading to Tswassen and we were parked at the side of the boat. I was sitting in the driver's seat of my Toyota 4Runner with the door open, bare feet up on the seat painting my toenails. I snapped a selfie showing my toes with kleenex in between, bottle of nail polish in my hand, with the ferry railings and ocean behind me. By the way, I'm really, REALLY good at selfies. Sure enough, I nailed the shot. I wrote a caption that started with listing some of the hardest things I had to do to become more successful: door knocking (yes, I did this when I started working for the investment firm), courses, exams, getting fired, writing a book. Then I wrapped it up with a huge dose of *gratitude:*

*"All of this stuff was really hard. When I was going through it, there was no way I was going to admit it was hard because I*

*wouldn't even let myself believe it was hard for fear I would lose my momentum. I was in my "fake it til I make it" phase. And now I feel ready to share that it was all really, really hard, but I am so glad I did it because it led me to having the business and freedom I have today. And I want to thank all of you who have supported me along the way, especially all of my clients and my mom who lent me money more than a few times!!"*

I found my voice on social media that summer. Then two years later, I sat in a cabin on my solo writing retreat, writing my next book called *"Find Your Voice On Social Media".*

I found my voice because I discovered my message:

**When you work hard focused on the specific lifestyle you want, you will achieve it.**

The funny thing is, I thought I wanted to enjoy a "selfish summer", but it turned out that I didn't want that. It's the same for every business owner who finds their niche: it takes working with the wrong clients to better understand who they are supposed to be working with.

Before all the road tripping and ferry rides and beach time, my selfish summer began with five days of volunteering at a summer camp. I went to summer camp as a child and my cabin leaders had a huge impact on my life. I wanted to provide that experience for young girls once I was an adult, but it didn't happen in my twenties because I was too busy partying, raising my son and paying my bills.

As I came to the end of my selfish summer, I looked back at where it began: at summer camp. I knew that's where I wanted to be for half of my next few summers.

Now it's your turn to write stories from your life: the people and random, or not so random, happenings which led you to discovering your purpose. Some of your most powerful stories are buried deep, or you may not realize how powerful they are until you take time today and this week to answer these questions and see where your memory takes you...

## Milestone 1 final step: Nine Stories

Write 3 stories for each question in Google Docs. (If you don't know how to use Google Docs, instructions are coming in the next chapter.)

1. What **challenges** did you face that led you to finding more clarity or a better understanding of your purpose?

2. Who are the most **influential people** in your life and how did they make you a better person?

3. Describe your greatest **pinch me moments**; achievements, client success stories and dreams come true.

If you're having trouble digging up the most valuable lessons you have ever learned, the stuff that makes you YOU, try using your Facebook or Instagram profile to help you. If you're like me and you've been posting about your life for 10+ years, let the photos from your life remind you of your greatest challenges, influential people and pinch me moments.

*"Why do I have to write Nine Stories about myself? I thought this wasn't about me…"*

Great question, and I've heard this question/objection many times. The simple answer is:

**You have to write nine stories from your life because storytelling works.**

Stories spark emotion, and it's <u>emotion</u> that drives people to take action, or at the very least, remember <u>who told the story</u> that sparked the emotion.

Here are two examples of how storytelling will work for you to attract your niche people:

**Pre-book launch storytelling on social media:** The best way to find the people who need your book, even before it is finished, is by sharing some of your most impactful life events and lessons learned on social media. People who can relate to your life stories will remember you and spread the word about your upcoming book.

**Sharing stories in your book:** The best way to help your readers understand and remember the key concepts in your book is through storytelling. It's like looking at a page of only words compared to a children's book with fun and colourful illustrations. You're literally painting a picture for them when you give an example of a step or mindset in story form.

# Social Media Post Challenge:
## <u>Gratitude</u>

Do you want to feel some "Gratitude Marketing Magic"? Open your phone and choose a photo of you doing something you love, perhaps on vacation, or hiking, or at the opera. Post the image on social media with a caption about one of your "Nine Stories". End your story with a few sentences about **why you're grateful** for the challenge/mentor/win that led you to that experience.

## Connect a story to each *Essential Topic* in your book

Coming up in Milestone 2, you will build a bullet point list of the most valuable lessons, concepts, and mindsets your readers absolutely must know when they are done reading your book. **This list is called your "Essential Topics".**

If you like the idea of starting with writing your *Essential Topics* before your Nine Stories, or working on them simultaneously, go for it. But make sure you have all nine stories written before moving on to Milestone 3. You will need these valuable, powerful stories from your life to complete the marketing and lead magnet steps coming up.

## Stop, drop and write

Do everything in your power to say *YES* to creativity when it knocks.

When I think of an important message I want to share with Fempreneurs, I either STOP, DROP AND WRITE, or I grab my phone and use the voice recorder. I hope you will do the same for your people.

WRITE YOUR DAMN BOOK, WOMAN!   BY LYNDSIE BARRIE

# Chapter 5:
# Knowledge is powerless without ACTION

How will you guide your readers from READING to DOING?

Think back to how you achieved the outcome(s) your readers are looking for, or the steps you've helped your clients take. Guide your readers through what they will have to actually DO to achieve their desired outcome. They can't just read about it.

It's not enough to hear stories about others experiencing the positive change you want.

Fempreneurs often have workshop material, checklists and mini guides they've created which can easily be repurposed into a book chapter. If you are a coach or mentor, or you have created a course or led a workshop, the **Action Steps** or **Homework** you have your attendees complete will be useful for the next writing exercise. But if you haven't created learning material for your business, you're about to.

Describe three key challenges your readers are facing that you can help them overcome.

Examples from my business:

1. I want to learn how to attractively package and price my smart brain.

2. I need a social media marketing plan and a clear message.

3. I need to get over my fear of shooting and posting videos of myself on Instagram.

☐ Write any three challenges your readers are facing that you can help them overcome in your notebook. Check the box when it's done.

Next, for each challenge, write an action plan with 4-5 steps to get them moving in the right direction. For example, I created the "Video Marketing Checklist" to help women shoot and post quick and engaging videos. It's a tool I give to workshop attendees and it's a free gift on my website.

Here's another example of how I addressed a common challenge I heard from female coaches and practitioners in the wellness industry: By teaching a workshop about *"How to attractively package and price your smart brain"*. This is the action plan I walk my workshop attendees through, and this is how you will map out your action plan in a moment:

## WORKSHOP:
## HOW TO ATTRACTIVELY PACKAGE
## AND PRICE YOUR SMART BRAIN

**Step One**
Complete the "Message Clarification Tool" handout.
*(It is coming in Milestone 3, and you can find it at yycfempreneurs.com/authors.)*

## Step Two
Build a survey at <u>mailchimp.com</u> to find out which are the top 3 wellness problems and how to help solve them.

## Step Three
Give survey respondents a FREE ticket to a virtual wellness workshop/class on Google Meet.

## Step Four
Post on social media about this FREE GIFT and how they can get it, *"by taking my 2 minute wellness survey"*, every other day for the 2-3 weeks leading up to the FREE workshop/class (the free workshop IS the free gift).

## Step Five
Offer workshop attendees two offers: a low/medium priced offer <u>and</u> a higher priced offer with a time sensitive 20% discount (2-3 days).

This step involves brainstorming and building two offers. This is the **MEATIEST** part because this is why they came to the workshop: *to learn how to package and price their smart brain.*

Write your action plans:

---

**Action Plan 1:**

Step 1

Step 2

Step 3

Step 4

Step 5

---

**Action Plan 2:**

Step 1

Step 2

Step 3

Step 4

Step 5

**Action Plan 3:**

Step 1

Step 2

Step 3

Step 4

Step 5

# What will you offer your readers for continued support?

Begin thinking about whether or not you want to mention products, coaching or services in your book which your readers can learn more about on your website. For example, all of my books talk about the six week marketing school I offer. I also mention my business coaching and website design services. If you are open to providing your readers with support, or you have helpful products/tools available for purchase, let them know!

## Your three offers are their *Natural Next Steps*

Do you have three offers right now? The offers are your niche people's WAYS TO TAKE ACTION - their *natural next steps.*

What would I find on your website under the **Services** or **Events** tab? And would I find a free gift/lead magnet so I can get a little taste of how you improve lives?

It's our job as entrepreneurs to provide three *natural next steps* for our ideal clients.

For most entrepreneurs, myself included, we have to throw lots of spaghetti at the wall before it sticks. My three natural next steps for Fempreneurs became clear after giving lots of time and knowledge away for free and getting feedback.

*\*\*\*Getting feedback is the most important part, otherwise there is no way to learn what our niche people want from us!*

Giving time and knowledge away for free is something I do less and less every year, but I'll never stop completely because:

OFFERING MY TIME AND KNOWLEDGE FOR FREE IS THE BEST WAY TO MEET NEW FEMPRENEURS WHO WANT TO TAKE MY *NATURAL NEXT STEPS.*

The free gift/lead magnet strategy works. Plain and simple. Anyone who has ever told you that business owners should NEVER give their knowledge or time away for free is just plain wrong. This false belief comes from a scarcity mindset. Instead, choose to have an abundance mindset.

However, the free gift/lead magnet strategy will only result in you earning more money from your talents if you have 2-3 attractively packaged offers at varying price points. These are your *natural next steps.*

Do not have 5-10 offers/natural next steps on your website. It's too many. You should have only three.

## Offer #1: FREE

This is a MUST when packaging and pricing your smart brain, even when it's a free offer:

**SCURGENCY.** This is *scarcity* and *urgency* combined.

For example, on my website the first thing you'll find below my welcome video is a button that says FREE CLASS. Go take a look now at yycfempreneurs.com and sign up if you haven't attended my free class before.

There is SCURGENCY mixed into this free class offer because it happens only six times a year on Google Meet and people must attend live. I do not send out the recording.

Right now this free class is the main way I am growing my email list and meeting new Fempreneurs who want to see how I can help them.

When they register for my free class, they immediately receive an email with a surprise free gift: 2-3 steps they can take today to improve their marketing. Because I have written many books for Fempreneurs, I have tons of content I can quickly repurpose into a surprise free gift. I refresh the email after every free video class, six times each year.

We'll talk about your two paid offers in a moment, but first I want to make sure you understand how to use your *free gift* as an online *lead magnet.*

# How to attract leads online

Note: this is an overview of my **lead magnet system**. I want to make sure so you understand how it works before you continue putting the system in place.

1.  Clearly identify the goal for your lead magnet. There is only one option when you follow my lead magnet system, and that is TO GROW A NICHE EMAIL LIST.

2.  Set a timeline for your lead magnet: when the free gift will expire, or when the free class/event will happen. Marketing a lead magnet for 3 weeks is ideal.

3.  Set up your sign up form at mailchimp.com. Ask 2-3 questions in the sign up form so they feel like this is 100% about you helping them solve a problem - never about you growing your email list or selling to them. These questions are also how you get feedback on your ideas and get to know your niche people better.

4.  Set up the automated email which contains the free gift. Get a few people to proofread your sign up page and automated email before you begin marketing your free gift.

5.  Embed the sign up page link in a button on your website that says FREE GIFT or FREE CLASS. Make sure to indicate the date it will no longer be available, or the date of the free class. This is your SCURGENCY.

6.  Have a few people test the technology to make sure the button works and the automated email sends.

7. Now it's time for your lead magnet to start attracting your niche people on social media. The best way to explain how your free gift will help them is... YES! YOU'RE CORRECT - VIDEO!!! Shoot a few different videos, each with slightly different wording, so they're ready in your phone for posting later. Use the "Book Purpose Sentence", but make it for the free gift/class.

8. Your free gift marketing includes your clear and powerful message with SCURGENCY, and directs people to your website to sign up. Talk about your free gift every other day on social media, being mindful not to talk ONLY about this free gift. Use the 4 Types of Posts tool to keep your audience engaged and growing. Mix up the ways you post about the free gift on Instagram/Facebook, switching between regular posts and reels, and a mix of videos and images.

9. Capture the FREE marketing power of Instagram stories! Stories have the best conversion rate for two reasons: stories are viewed more than regular posts on Instagram, and we can add a link. If you don't know how to do this, Google it or ask someone who is Instagram savvy.

10. BOOST: After a week of posting about your free gift, choose a post that's not a reel and tap "View Insights" (on Facebook or Instagram). Notice the engagement numbers. Look at all the posts and choose the one that has the highest "organic engagement", meaning you did not pay to "boost" it. **Boost the post** to attract people who don't follow you. (Depending on your

financial situation, invest in a boost for 7 days at $5-$10/day.)

11. After 7 days you should have at least a few new email subscribers at mailchimp.com (people who said yes to your free gift.) If you have zero sign ups after posting about it a few times, try the previous step (BOOST) for a few days. If this is your first time offering a lead magnet, don't feel discouraged, because: "CRICKETS" DON'T MEAN "NO". THEY MEAN, "NOT RIGHT NOW", OR "NOT LIKE THAT". If there are still no takers after a few BOOST days, get some help with clarifying your message.

12. When people sign up, look at their name and answers by logging into mailchimp.com and clicking on "Audience". Try to find them on social media so you can send them a message like this, or even better, a video of you saying:

*"<Name>, thank you so much for signing up for my free <industry word> class! I see that you said in the sign up form that you are really looking forward to learning how to <insert their answer>..."*

Next I ask them for more info about their answer. For example, when people sign up for my free video marketing class I ask the questions on the next page...

This is a screenshot from the sign up form embedded in the FREE CLASS button at yycfempreneurs.com:

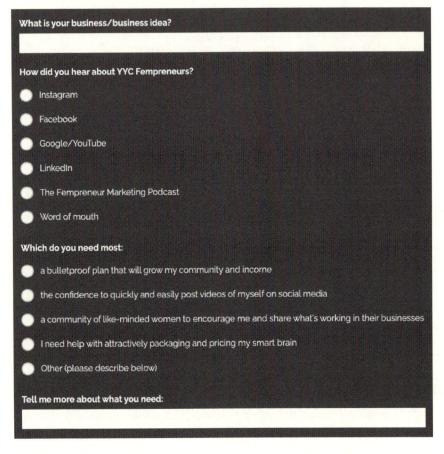

A lead magnet strategy is 10x more profitable when you:

1. Strike up REAL conversations with your new leads

2. Provide two natural next steps at two different price points

For example, soon you will set up the **Upcoming Book Lead Magnet System**. This is where you give away a free draft chapter of your book in exchange for survey responses (market research for your book). When you see in your mailchimp account that someone has signed up to receive a draft chapter of your upcoming book, you will strike up a meaningful conversation with them either by messaging them on social media, or by sending them an email. The key is to make it about them. Let them know you read their answers to your survey, you are so excited to hear their feedback on your draft chapter, and address any questions or ideas for your book they shared in the survey. As the conversation continues, and if they are WOWed by you, they will head to your website to find *natural next steps.*

Throughout the remainder of this book I'll walk you through my **Upcoming Book Lead Magnet System** so you are continually attracting more and more people who want to read your upcoming book.

# Your paid natural next steps

You won't talk specifically about them in your book, but it's important to build two paid offers if you don't currently have them. While writing your book, and after your book is complete, people will discover you and want to learn more about you. Without these two offers, you'll miss out on working with more of your ideal clients. If you have too many offers, people will feel confused and no longer WOWed by you.

**Here's an example of how I position my two paid natural next steps in a live workshop:**

At the beginning of my workshop, part of my introduction is sharing that I offer group and 1:1 training for wellness practitioners and coaches seeking more online credibility and an effective lead magnet system. The lower price option is a six week group training program. The higher price is a

1:1 coaching program. I would position the offers like this throughout my workshop:

Beginning
A brief mention of the two offers with emphasis on their desired outcome: *"Today I'll share a few of my best marketing and income building strategies. Later in the workshop I'll offer a couple ways you can gain even more online credibility and new clients."*

Middle
Attach numbers to the two offers and describe their ideal outcome differently: *"If you're someone who needs 1:1 guidance and accountability, I hope you'll consider joining my six week marketing school. Or we can look at working together for a few months to clarify your online message and attract more of your niche people."*

End
Ask a powerful question and wrap up with a time-sensitive offer: *"Do you want to learn how to earn more money from your talents with my help? I have two opportunities for you, both of which are 20% off for the next 48 hours..."*

*If you don't already have two offers, or if you have more than two offers, grab your pen and notebook now. Get to work building your two offers.*

## How to set up Google Drive and Google Docs

If you've been using Gmail for a while and understand how to use Google Drive and Docs, you can skip this next part.

Use Google Drive to store your writing documents, or "Docs". Think of Google Drive as a filing cabinet drawer, and Docs is the file folder containing your pages of writing.

On your computer, open your web browser (Safari or Chrome) and go to <u>drive.google.com</u> to set up your "Drive", or filing cabinet drawer, for your new book.

Click "New" and then "Google Docs":

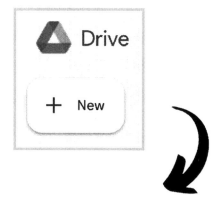

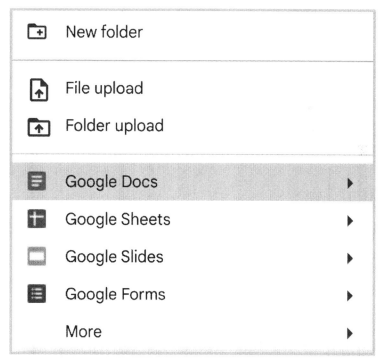

To complete Milestone 1, you will write your Nine Stories in Google Docs. Then to complete Milestone 2, you will add two more Docs, like this:

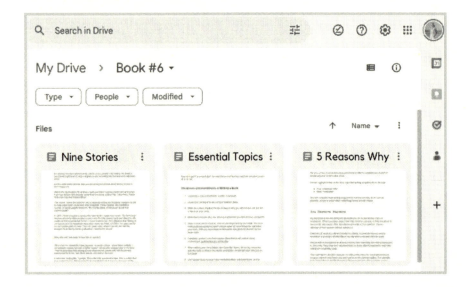

Once you have checked all the boxes on page 54, that's it for Milestone 1. Congratulations on everything you've accomplished so far!

I have some really exciting news for you:

It's time to start marketing your upcoming book using the **checklist on pages 69-70!**

Put on your **favourite pump-up song** and play it LOUD as you read your new weekly social media marketing tasks and begin Milestone 2!

## Write your *Essential Topics* in Google Docs

This is a bullet point list of the most valuable lessons, concepts, and mindsets your readers absolutely must know when they are done reading your book. Once you've typed it in Google Docs, check the box on page 55.

## Build your *Book Framework* - write it in your notebook

Begin drawing a map of where you will take your readers. Basically you're building draft chapters by grouping together similar topics and organizing steps and topics in the best order. It should look something like this in your notebook when you start:

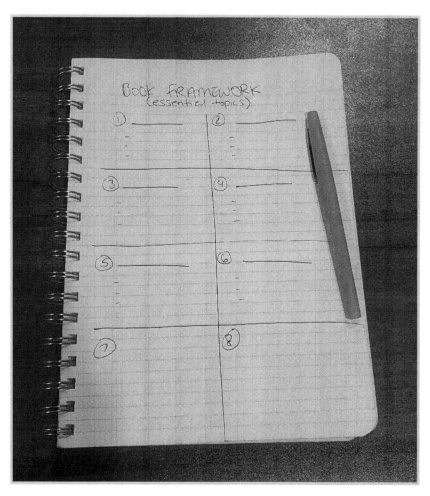

After adding the *Essential Topics* to your *Book Framework,* it should look like this:

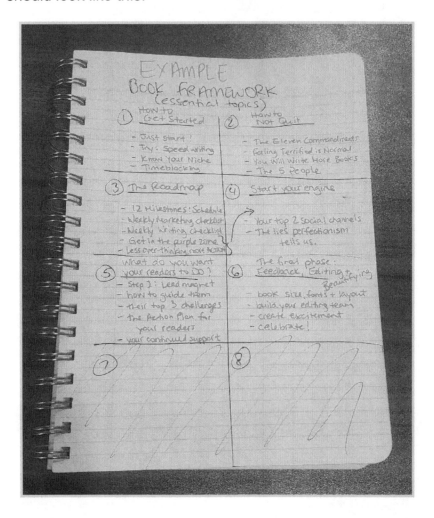

## Write *My 5 Reasons Why* in Google Docs

These are the top 5 reasons why you will complete this book. Go back and read what you wrote at the end of chapter 2 about what it would feel like to quit and who you would let down. Then write the top 5 reasons why you're all-in, no matter what.

# Post one of your *Nine Stories* or a draft chapter of your book on your blog

Again, if you don't have a website, you can use Facebook or LinkedIn as a place to publish your writing.

For your first blog, choose a story that illustrates <u>why you are writing a book.</u> This is another big marketing step, just like telling the world that you are writing a book. It's normal to be nervous, but like Felicia said, do it anyway. It's worth it.

If you are concerned about spelling or grammar, have someone proofread your story before posting it on the world wide web. Use the steps below…

# Proofreaders, please!

Posting your writing on the internet will be less scary if you've had a couple sets of eyes go over it first. This is another reason why I love Google Docs: it's a great proofreading tool, both on its own and for sending to *human proofreaders.*

While typing your Nine Stories in Google Docs, did you see a few of those squiggly lines under your spelling or grammar mistakes? If not, you're a better writer than I am. Now that you have fixed the squiggly lines, do you want a human or two to read your story and let you know if anything is confusing? I do suggest you take this step because the feedback and ideas from proofreaders can be priceless.

Here's how to get the help you're looking for using Google Docs:

<u>Start with choosing three human proofreaders.</u> It's likely only 1-2 of these people will come through for you, because

people are busy. You really only need one person to actually read your story and provide honest feedback.

Create a Google Docs for each of your proofreaders. Name them "**Suzy** *(her name, not yours)* **Proofreading Nov 23rd** *(the date I'd like it done by)*". Copy and paste the story into each Docs and then click "Share".

**Make sure to set permissions to "Commenter" so you can see the changes they made and learn from them:**

Share Suzy's Docs with Suzy, Marg's with Marg, and so on. You don't want them all commenting in the same Docs.

# Random thoughts and encouragement

Earlier today while writing this book, I did three things that gave me a surge of creativity. I hope you find them helpful. Here they are:

My writing mojo was dwindling, so I decided to **RELOCATE** from my office, which is in the basement. I usually prefer to work at the kitchen table, but up until an hour ago I had to be in my basement office because the house was busy. But it's just me here for the next few hours so I have relocated to the kitchen table.

Actually, I don't really have a *preferred* work station when it comes to writing. What I know for sure is I need to change up my surroundings every day. While writing this book I moved back and forth between my basement office and kitchen table whenever my writing mojo decreased, or when my chair became uncomfortable.

The second thing I did earlier today to boost my writing mojo was…

**GET A LITTLE SWEATY.** I did some downward-dogs, alternating pushing my heels to the ground, then ten pushups from my knees, then a child's pose, then some squats and more push ups. I refilled my water bottle too.

The last thing I did was **GRAB A MOTIVATING BOOK** and stood by the big south-facing sliding glass door off the kitchen to feel the **sunshine** on my face as I read. I randomly opened it and read a few pages. It was a story about a man who was whining that he hadn't achieved the success he felt he should have after persevering as long as he had. He compared himself to people similar to him who had not worked harder or longer than he had, but were wildly successful. The advice given to him was impeccable: QUIT. *If you don't love the work you do, then why do it? Quit. And if* *after a few months or years you actually miss it and want to return, then do that. But right now, it's obvious you are not loving the path you've chosen and haven't been for quite some time.*

So that got me thinking: I am so grateful that I don't feel like that about anything I've done or am currently working on. I love that I feel excited to write after a few days away, and that writing brings me so much joy. I truly feel blessed to have this opportunity to be writing another book for women. Sometimes it amazes me that I still enjoy the challenging moments when it's hard to explain the techy steps in one of my processes. I can't imagine having expectations of this creative process, or being surrounded by people telling me I should be achieving more status or wealth from my writing. Words can't express how grateful I am to be able to share these stories, mindsets and my book writing process with you, simply because I enjoy it.

I just wanted you to know all that, because I don't think I have told you nearly enough how much I have loved writing this book, even when I'm behind schedule like I am right now!

It's such a huge gift to be able to do something you love with your time and energy. Please don't take it for granted as you write your book.

In the moments when your writing mojo is dwindling, or you're starting back after a few days away from writing and the words are not flowing, try this:

## Push the "Reset" Button

1. Relocate to a different room in your home. Or to a coffee shop, or an airbnb!

2. Move your body, woman!

3. Read a few pages of ANY motivating book!

Alright! Let's continue… Did you check all the boxes on page 55? If so,

## Welcome to Milestone 3

In chapter 1 you began clarifying your message by writing your **Book Purpose Sentence**. Now it's time to do it again and notice if anything has changed or become more clear:

This book helps (who)

learn/do (what they'll learn/do)

so they can (their desired outcome)

As you share your "Book Purpose" sentence once or twice a week on social media your niche people's ears will perk up. This is a huge step in the right direction, *but what you do next is crucial.*

## THE ULTIMATE CONVERSATION OPENER: *"May I have your opinion on...?"*

This is where the survey comes in. The #1 purpose of your survey is to show your niche people you care about solving their problem. Furthermore, you are reaching out to better understand the problem so you can write a super helpful book about it.

In your survey you will use words they associate with their problem, and just like me back at that conference looking up at my future business coach, they will feel like you get them. They will view you as an expert in your field **whether or not they actually complete your survey.**

That last part is important, so I'll repeat it: **do not measure your survey success on how many people complete your survey.**

Writing a survey will give you clarity for your book and marketing momentum even if ZERO PEOPLE TAKE YOUR SURVEY.

In your survey you will ask your niche people to describe:

- their problem

- how they want it solved

- how they will feel when the problem is solved

Think about the most important topics and mindsets you can't wait to share in your book. It's a good idea to jot them down in your notebook as they come to you right now, or add them to your *Essential Topics* list.

Now think about why these topics and mindsets actually matter. What value do they have? How will your readers' lives be better once they do or learn them?

Prepare to craft your survey questions by answering the following:

**Write 3-5 ideal outcomes you can help your niche people achieve:**

*What's holding them back from achieving their desired outcome? Write 3-5 roadblocks you can help them smash through:*

# Craft your survey questions

You can write out your survey questions first in your notebook, or you can skip that step and go straight to building your survey at mailchimp.com.

If you feel confused or stuck, watch the survey creation video at yycfempreneurs.com/author.

Start your survey with a brief intro like this:

> *"Hello! My name is Lyndsie and I'm writing a book for Fempreneurs who want to build social media confidence so they can attract more of the right clients. To thank you for sharing your ideas and feedback in this survey, I'll send you a FREE draft chapter of my upcoming book."*

These are your survey questions:

**1. Which part of (your industry word) would you like to learn about most?** (Multiple choice.)

Example: Which part of social media marketing would you like to learn about most?

- Writing engaging captions
- Shooting and posting videos QUICKLY
- Clarifying my message
- How to turn social media followers into paying clients

**2. What's holding you back from** *(your industry word)*?
(Multiple choice.)

Example: What's holding you back from feeling confident on social media?

- Comparing myself to others
- Not tech-savvy enough
- I don't have a plan to follow
- I don't have a team of like-minded ladies to bounce ideas off of

**3. Which of the following would you find most helpful:**
(Multiple choice.)

Example:

- A video marketing checklist
- A step-by-step guide for planning social media marketing content
- A tool or writing exercise to help me clarify my message
- A list of mantras to boost my confidence

**4. Describe any other** *(your industry word)* **solutions you would like me to include in the book:** (Text box.)

Example: Describe any other social media marketing solutions you are looking for:

***Always put the text box last, after clearly communicating: *"I understand this topic and I am here to help you!"*

Your last survey building step is to add the following fields to your survey:

- first name
- last name
- email - and make sure to toggle "Required" and "Ask to subscribe" to "ON".

The default checkbox text says "Subscribe me to your newsletter", which is not what they are doing, plus no one wants to read a newsletter EVER. So change the text to something like, *"Yes! Please send me draft chapters of the upcoming book."*

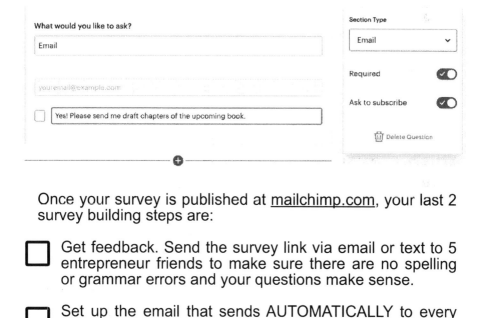

Once your survey is published at mailchimp.com, your last 2 survey building steps are:

☐ Get feedback. Send the survey link via email or text to 5 entrepreneur friends to make sure there are no spelling or grammar errors and your questions make sense.

☐ Set up the email that sends AUTOMATICALLY to every person who takes your survey and checks the "Yes!" box. Instructions are at yycfempreneurs.com/author.

Check the boxes once these steps are complete. If all the Milestone 3 boxes are checked on page 56, move on to Milestone 4.

What are you most excited about right now?

Are you picturing yourself holding your book, feeling overjoyed and so proud? Or perhaps you have children and you can't wait to show them that anything is possible.

It was a really exciting moment when I walked in the doors at Indigo in Calgary and saw Tiana sitting at her book signing table. Then I captured this *ussie* so I could share it with you...

Tiana joined my FemAuthors group in late 2021 and her book was completed in June 2022. She's a wife and a mom to three busy boys. One of my favourite things about Tiana is she does what she says she will do.

# Tips for Becoming An Author from Tiana Fech

<u>Tiana, how did it feel to complete your book?</u>

*Completing my book felt unbelievable! It was something that I had wanted to do for a long time and, with the support of an awesome community, I made it happen. Holding a copy of my book in my hands made me feel an incredible sense of pride and accomplishment.*

<u>How did you celebrate the completion of your book?</u>

*I had the amazing opportunity to be a part of the FEMTalks event held at the ATB Entrepreneur Centre in Calgary, Alberta with 3 other incredible female authors and entrepreneurs. The event included networking, free copies of each of our books, a 20 minute talk from each of us about our areas of expertise, and refreshments, of course! There was even an after party held at a local pub! We had over 30 attendees at this event along with lots of positive energy, connections, and feedback. I'm so grateful for this opportunity to celebrate with such an amazing group.*

*During my presentation at this event, I asked the attendees to think about their answer to the question: Who is your favourite teacher and why does this person stand out for you? When we opened up the floor for key takeaways and questions, one woman shared who her favourite teacher was and that it happened to be the person that she was attending the event with! She talked about how her friend really took her under her wing when they started working together and how she continued to demonstrate care and interest in her life outside of the job itself. Her friend helped her to foster her passions and to build upon them. This was truly one of my biggest highlights and most touching moments from the event that day.*

## Tell us a story about one of the best connections you made because of your book and how it has helped your career.

*One of the best connections that I made through writing my book is Felicia Yap (also featured in this book). Our shared Author experience introduced us to one another. I hired Felicia to help me improve my video content for my podcast called The People Teaching People Podcast. We ended up having a great connection and attended a networking event for female entrepreneurs together. Felicia is an incredible heart-centred business owner (and mom of three!) and I look forward to continuing to learn from her, supporting her with her business in any way that I can, and growing our friendship. I am thrilled that she agreed to be a guest on an episode of my podcast!*

## How is your business different now that you're an Author?

*My book has become my 'above and beyond' business card that I can gift, donate, sell and use as a tool for people to get to know me and how I can serve and support them. My book is not only on Amazon but it is also in a local Indigo store where I have an upcoming book signing scheduled! It has led to speaking opportunities at events and on podcasts, new business connections, referrals, and new clients. I send each of my small business clients a copy of my book which allows us to use our time together more efficiently because it serves as a reference guide and workbook for the development of their online (or in-person) learning experience.*

*I use a relationship-centred approach in the work that I do as a learning development consultant helping businesses create courses and optimize programs. I believe that both education and business are truly all about relationships. Becoming an Author has proved to be an incredible way to build relationships and my business network. I have had people share with me, through conversation and on social media, how they have gifted my book to their friends and clients. I have had people reach out to me to let me know how much my book has helped them with developing their learning experiences. I have also had clients hire me to work with them one-on-one as a consultant as a result of them being 'introduced' to me through my book!*

## How is your personal life different now that you're an Author?

*As a mom of three boys, life can be a bit of a juggle. I am always looking for ways to work as efficiently as possible so that I can be present and engaged with my family. My book has proved to be a tool to do just that because it allows me to support my clients with more ease. I can easily reference pages and chapters of my book when clients ask questions and I can also have them refer to sections prior to our one-on-one sessions so that we can truly make the most of our time together.*

*Becoming an Author has also resulted in my kids seeing their mom have an idea and a dream and then making it happen. I felt a huge sense of pride taking my family into Indigo and showing them my book on the bookshelf! I hope that it inspires them to take action and to live their dreams even if they seem scary, challenging, and beyond the realm of possibility.*

## Tiana's Top 5 Tips for completing a book:

1. **Block off time.** *I had to be intentional about creating time and space in my schedule to write my book. I had to make it a priority.*

2. **Find accountability buddies.** *Being connected with a group of people who were also writing a book helped me to stay committed to my end goal and provided an incredible source of motivation and inspiration.*

3. **Look back at your existing content.** *I looked back at my previous social media posts, podcast show notes, workshops, blog posts, client projects etc. to generate ideas and get the juices flowing. You don't have to start from scratch!*

4. **Talk about your book.** *When I shared that I was writing a book and put it out into the world, it felt more real and made me feel even more committed to bringing it to fruition. It was also an opportunity to take my community along the journey of writing my book with me because ultimately, it was for them!*

5. **Ask for help.** *When I hit a roadblock with writing, organizing, editing, designing my book cover, or really anything along the way, I reached out to my community. Not doing this would have made it really easy to stay stuck and not get my book out into the world. When I needed inspiration or direction for my book, I asked my people what they wanted to know or to learn more about. I reflected on the FAQs asked by my clients and community.*

## Lastly, what was one of the most difficult parts of writing a book?

The most difficult part of writing a book was getting started. It seemed like such a daunting, overwhelming, impossible goal. I remember thinking that life was busy enough and how would I be able to find the time in my schedule to write a book!? Of course, we make time for the things that are important to us. This meant that I had to make writing my book a priority. The first thing that I did was join an accountability group. The FemAuthors group led by Lyndsie Barrie included an incredible group of women who each shared the common goal of writing and self-publishing a book. At our first session Lyndsie had us brainstorming and idea generating. She encouraged us to think about frequently asked questions and reach out to our community for their feedback on the topics they would want to read about in our book. Slowly but surely I developed an initial outline. I took my outline and created a timeline for myself with completion dates for each chapter of my book, editing, cover design, and submission to Amazon. I scheduled writing time into my calendar and made it a non-negotiable appointment and not something that I could bump to the bottom of the list, or pardon the pun, write off. As I worked away at my book, there were times where I got stuck and hit a roadblock. In these moments, I made sure to reach out to my accountability group, community, and family and friends for help, advice, and direction. One word at a time, one sentence at a time, one paragraph at a time, my book went from an idea in my head to completion!

***Hear Tiana share more of her book writing and marketing stories on The Fempreneur Podcast and check out Tiana's Podcast: "People Teaching People."*

WRITE YOUR DAMN BOOK, WOMAN!  BY LYNDSIE BARRIE

# Chapter 6:
# Everything you need to know about marketing your upcoming book

Now it's time to finish setting up your "Upcoming Book" Lead Magnet System. This is how we move our niche people up the "Relationship-Ometer".

I'll illustrate how the "Relationship-Ometer" works in this 3 step example:

1.  Sally sees a post you boosted on Instagram about your upcoming book, likes what she sees and follows you. She's now at <u>level one</u> on the Relationship-Ometer.

2.  Sally sees a video you posted on your story inviting people to read a free draft chapter of your upcoming book. She clicks the link in your story and lands on your website. There she sees a button that says FREE GIFT, so she clicks it.

***Level two is tricky.** Sally doesn't need to actually receive your free draft chapter to be at level two. All she needs to do to move up on your Relationship-Ometer is "click" on your Instagram story (or link in your bio) and take a quick* peek at your website. *This is what makes it tricky: you don't know how many people are at level two. You only know who is at level three…*

3.   Sally says "Yes please!" to your free gift by filling out the form at mailchimp.com, which is where your FREE GIFT button takes her. She then automatically receives the free chapter via email. Even if she doesn't open the email, <u>Sally is at level three on your Relationship-Ometer.</u>

In the remainder of the book I'll walk you through how to get as many people as possible to Level 3 on your Relationship-Ometer. Many of them will move up to levels 4 and 5 if you have two paid offers clearly available on your website. These are the "natural next steps" we talked about in chapter 5.

Moving more of your niche people up your Relationship-Ometer is WHY YOU ARE ON SOCIAL MEDIA. Finding people who want to read your book and pointing them towards joining your email list is what it's all about.

## Moving people up the Relationship-Ometer IS Marketing - they are the same thing

We move our niche people up the Relationship-Ometer by *making it about them.* We offer them something they want for free, give it to them, then follow up and ask for their feedback on, in this case, the free draft chapter of the upcoming book.

**Spoiler alert:** asking for feedback on your draft chapters will result in your niche people moving up to <u>Level 4 on your Relationship-Ometer</u>. Yay!!

This whole process starts with sharing your clear book purpose message on social media, then offering a free sneak peek of your upcoming book with clear directions for how to get it. Now let's make sure they can actually get from your social channel to your website by completing the first "techy" step in Milestone 4:

> ☐ **Add a FREE GIFT button to your website home page, if you have a website (button links to survey).**

## Welcome to Milestone 4!

***If you don't have a website, you will still complete the same "techy" steps, but it will look a little bit different. Instead of posting your survey to your website, you will post the survey link on Facebook, LinkedIn and/or your Instagram bio.

If you don't have a website, skip to the instructions for how to: *"Add the survey link to your Instagram bio",* on the next page.

Can you add a "free gift" button to your website yourself, or do you need to ask your website designer to do it?

I'm hoping you are using a platform like Squarespace or Wix, the best user-friendly website options I've found for DIY-ers like myself. If you can't do this yourself, this is how to ask your website designer to do this in an email:

*"I need a button on the top of my website home page that says 'FREE GIFT'.*

*Button link: (insert your mailchimp survey link here).*

*Above the button, I need one sentence of text that says: "(insert your 'Book Purpose' sentence). If you would like to read a draft chapter, click the button."*

Again, if you would like to see how this "lead magnet system" should look and work, go to yycfempreneurs.com and click on the purple button.

Here are some tips to help you complete Milestone 4 on schedule:

- If you don't know how to **add the survey link to your Instagram bio**, Google "How to change link Instagram Bio".

- A selfie will work great for the ***"May I have your opinion?"*** post. Try pointing up like I did on the cover of this book, and then add text to where you're pointing. Play around with camera angles and "pinching" your phone screen to zoom out so there's more room beside your head for the text.

## How to make your #Authorlife Goal Board

A cork board or bristle board from the dollar store works. Or feel free to put the checklists and sticky notes directly on your wall.

On the left side put your weekly marketing checklist and the weekly writing checklist. You can print these at yycfempreneurs.com/author.

On the right side put up your *Book Framework.* Sticky notes come in handy for this so you can rearrange topics and add deadline dates.

## We're going live!

In the **Weekly Marketing Checklist** I asked you to:

> **Interview a complimentary business owner on Instagram Live, YouTube Live, or Facebook Live.**

And before you ask, yes, it has to be a *LIVE* video.

The ripple effect from showing up in a live video will blow your mind, no matter how many followers you have, or how many the person you go live with has.

The reason why we want to do a live video with someone who is in a complimentary industry is to have a casual yet meaningful conversation about a topic that is relative to both of your ideal clients. The best way to do this is take turns asking each other a list of 3-5 questions.

Look at your list of *Essential Topics* and think about local business owners who would have stories and tips to share about one or more of the topics.

If you're feeling like it will <u>not</u> be a good move business-wise to do a live video with someone who could be considered your "competition", *let's nip that in the bud right now.*

**Community over competition. Always.**

The size of your income is directly correlated to the size of your niche community. If your community looks very similar to someone else's, the opportunities for collaboration are endless.

Labeling someone as your "competition" comes from a **scarcity mindset.** There are more than enough people who are both in "your niche" and "their niche" for either of you to serve 1% of them. *Ditch the scarcity mindset and trust in the ripple effect that comes from showing up in a live video with a complimentary business owner.*

Like everything you do, your videos are about the people watching. It's not about "me vs. them", or pointing out why you're better at what you do than a competitor. *It's about adding value to the viewer's lives.*

**Here's how you invite other entrepreneurs to hop on a live video with you:**

Tailor each invite to the person and their niche people, but make sure to be crystal clear that this is about creating valuable, helpful content. Let them know you're writing a book and following a "book marketing strategy" that includes live video. Give them compliments to explain why you chose them: "I admire the way you do _____...", or "I've always wanted to have a conversation with you because _____...".

How you contact them will make a huge difference. You don't want to seem like you're copying and pasting the same invite to 20 people. The best way is in a less than one minute video which you send via social media. For example, Instagram or Facebook chat/message.

Mention you will add 3-5 of the topics from your book so they can pick a few for the live video.

Your goal is to host a live video once every 2 weeks until your book is done.

Here are the questions I ask my guests on The Fempreneur Podcast (yycfempreneurs.com/podcast):

1.  How does your business improve lives?

2.  What's one of the hardest challenges you've had to face as a business owner?

3.  What would you tell your 10 year younger self?

4.  Do you have any free gifts or little tastes of what you do that people can check out on your website?

At the time I'm writing this, I'm using an app called Restream.io. It's not free, but it's very worth the investment if you plan to continue showing up in live videos at least once a month. Here's why: it allows you to broadcast live with one or more guests on more than one channel at a time. So you hit "start" and you and your guest are live on three social channels at the same time! It's amazing!! Right now I'm using it for Facebook, YouTube and LinkedIn. Then I use the recordings of these live interviews for my podcast.

***When I find helpful new apps or tips to help you with marketing your book online, I'll email them to you. Sign up to receive my latest Author Tips at yycfempreneurs.com/author.*

## A look ahead at Milestones 5 - 9

As you continue to market your upcoming book, don't forget to WRITE YOUR BOOK. Before you move on to Milestone 5, let's take a look at your writing progress.

First of all, CONGRATULATE YOURSELF FOR KILLING IT at marketing. You wouldn't be here, about to embark on Milestone 5, if you hadn't done some awesome marketing work. Take an hour or two to celebrate.

How helpful are you finding the **Writing Timeblock Checklist** on page 37? Have you printed it and put it up on your **#authorlife Goal Board**? If not, <u>DO THIS NOW.</u> <u>Then...</u>

☐ <u>Check this box.</u>

How many hours of writing have you made happen in the past 7 days? And what about the 7 days before that? Write your average number of hours of writing time per week here:

\_\_\_\_.

If you want that to be a different number going forward, write it here:

\_\_\_\_.

Estimate how many chapters you've written so far and look at how many of your *Essential Topics* are still in the queue. If I were you, I would update my *Book Framework* and add it to my goal board with a deadline date for each chapter that still needs to be written RIGHT NOW.

How many weeks did it take you to complete Milestones 1 through 4? Write how many weeks:

_____.

***From today onward your goal is to complete one milestone each week and write at least one full chapter each week until you complete Milestones 9-12.** Five weeks from now you want to be sending your final chapters to your editors. You won't write any new chapters during the last 3 weeks/Milestones 10, 11 and 12, because that's when you will focus on formatting your final book and marketing your book launch event.

Note: Your goal is to send 2-3 chapters to your editors three times, each time with a one week or less deadline. To say it another way, your goal is to write a book that has 7-9 chapters total, plus a brief intro and conclusion, and send three chapters to your editors three times, one week apart.

In Milestone 6 you will build your editing team and send them your first 2-3 chapters to get their feedback and suggestions for how to improve it. *Begin thinking about who you will ask to be on your editing team now.*

☐ *Write their names in your notebook, or on your goal board. Then check this box.*

## Are you curious about how many pages your book will have?

Start with finding out how many words you have written in Google Docs: **Click "Tools", and then "Word count".**

Once you know the word count so far, use the following table, comparing two books that I have written, to help you decide on which book size and formatting options will work best for you:

| Find Your Voice on Social Media | We Should Be Friends |
|---|---|
| • 6x9 inch book | • 5x8 inch book |
| • 170 pages | • 192 pages |
| • 11pt font | • 11pt font |
| • 1.5 spacing | • single spacing |
| • 28,000 words | • 45,000 words |

## You've arrived at Milestone 5

First, you will shoot 3 "Quick Win" videos about 3 of your *Essential Topics.* I suggest you start with sharing a personal story about when you were struggling with "X" and how you overcame it.

Remember to shoot and store the videos in your phone so they're ready to post according to your Weekly Marketing Checklist. Do not shoot using the Instagram app, or any other app that is not your phone's camera app.

Upload your 3 "Quick Win" videos one at a time 3 days in a row to your YouTube channel. If you don't have a YouTube channel, set it up. It's really simple. Go to youtube.com, login and click "Upload Video".

What I mean by a "Quick Win" is a simple tip or mindset, something that will give them a positive result - FAST. Don't give them a long list of to-do's. Keep it simple, then mention you have more where that came from on your blog and in your upcoming book.

Each of your blogs includes the link to your survey so your readers can easily join your email list. As soon as you have three people on your email list (yes, only three), it's time to send them something new: *a book sneak peek that you haven't shared publicly yet:*

> ☐ At mailchimp.com, email a brand new piece of writing to your new subscribers. Follow the instructions at yycfempreneurs.com/author to complete this step.

Now that you have a growing email list, you may be wondering, *what am I going to send these people to keep them interested so they don't click "unsubscribe"?*

It's the same as social media: you will send them different forms of helpful content including stories, event invites and quick wins.

***Sending a video in every second to third email is the best way to keep them engaged.

**BONUS Marketing Challenge:** I encourage you to include one of your "Quick Win" videos in every other email and blog post. Do this by uploading each video to youtube.com, then embed the video link.

## How do you feel about continuing to show up in videos online?

If you're feeling less than "video confident", you're normal. Most people don't get as excited as I do about making videos. But that's not an excuse to stay stuck. There are quick and simple ways to gain video confidence.

If you're feeling like shooting videos is taking FOREVER, you're overthinking it. Let me help you by showing you how to shoot quick yet powerful videos to market your upcoming book:

There is a one hour video confidence course available at yycfempreneurs.com/author. It's extremely affordable and comes with a 100% money back guarantee. Set aside one hour and get it done today!

## How's the writing going?

Do you have a clear picture in mind of who you are writing a letter to each time you sit down at your computer? One thing I encourage my writing retreat attendees to do is give your reader a name. Decide how old she is, if she has kids, her hobbies and the specific problems you are helping her solve as she reads your book. Imagine you are writing a letter to this person.

If you're feeling like your writing is scattered, you're trying to talk to an audience that's too broad. You don't know who you're talking to.

You need to niche down.

## Is there such a thing as being "too niche"?

One of the key reasons why it is so important to talk specifically to a niche audience is that your message has more power. Delivering a super-duper niche message IS YOUR JOB. If you want to write a book that every single person can benefit from, and you want to market a book that is for EVERYONE, I can't help you.

If you're marketing to everyone, you're marketing to no one.

Was it difficult to write your "Book Purpose Sentence"?

If your audience is too broad, you can't describe how you can help them in one sentence.

Don't be afraid of being "too niche". There is no such thing. Your message will have maximum power when you are speaking to a niche audience.

## Milestone 6 - you're halfway there!

It's time to invite 6-10 editors to read and provide feedback on your book. You will also ask your editors to choose their favourite from a list of 3-4 title ideas. Follow these "Editor Invite" steps...

You can type the following editor invite script in an email or text message, but the best way is to say it in a video:

> *"Hello <name>. As you may have heard, I'm writing a book. I'm coming into the final phase of writing it and I'm looking for editors who want to help me, but will also shoot me straight, which is why I would really appreciate having you on my editing team. Your name will be listed as one of my editors on the first page of my book. If you can give me an hour of your time each week for the next three weeks, I'll send you the first third of my book to edit today. If you can have it edited one week from today, I'll send you the next third."*

WRITE YOUR DAMN BOOK, WOMAN! BY LYNDSIE BARRIE

Next you want to promise them a thank you gift. If they live near you, I suggest you take them for dinner and bring a little gift to the dinner, perhaps a notebook and one of your awesome pens, or anything you think they will like that will make them feel appreciated. If they don't live near you, promise to send them a $100 Amazon gift card (or more $$$ depending on your financial situation).

Next in your "Editor Invite" video (or email/text) let them know what their thank you gift will be: *"If I find your editing helpful, and you edit my entire book according to the deadlines, here's the thank you gift I want to give you: <tell them what it is>."*

Ask them to get back to you with an answer as soon as possible, and remind them it should take no more than one hour per week. Lastly, be so so so grateful for their time in advance if they decide to accept.

For each person who agrees to be an editor, follow these steps:

☐ On your computer go to docs.google.com

☐ Copy and paste the first 2-3 chapters that are ready for editing into a new Doc

☐ Title it with their name first, then "Book Editing" and share it to their email address

☐ Add to the top of the Docs: *"Thank you so much for editing my book! If you can have this first part edited by (deadline date - one week away), I'll send you the next chapters. Please type your suggestions into this Doc as I have an original copy. Don't be shy - edit anything you see that's not right: spelling, grammar, flow - I want all your suggestions!"*

150

☐ Ask the following feedback questions at the end of the Docs:

1. What was your favourite part?

2. How can I improve this section of my book?

3. What do you hope to read about later in this book?

☐ Google will email you each time they comment in the Docs. If they have not made any comments after 48 hours, politely nudge them in a text message. Or if they <u>have</u> started editing it, text them: *"Thank you so much for getting started! I appreciate you so much!!"*

Continue sending out the "Editor Invite" until you have a minimum of 4 people who are currently editing the first 2-3 chapters of your book.

## Milestone 6 - final step

Write down the names of any Authors you know who would be willing to "skim" (or fully read) your manuscript and provide you with a testimonial for the first page of your book and/or in your book marketing:

_____

_____

_____

_____

Asking Authors for testimonials is an optional step that's not listed in any of the milestones. If you choose to send your final manuscript PDF to each of the Authors, you can do so even if you still have a chapter or two to write. Or you can wait until your book has been uploaded to Amazon and send them the same PDF file.

Although it's not necessary, I do recommend you send your book PDF to the Authors you wrote on the last page.

**How did you feel about this at the end of Milestone 7...**

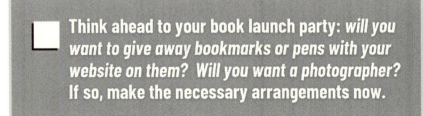

□ **Think ahead to your book launch party:** *will you want to give away bookmarks or pens with your website on them? Will you want a photographer? If so, make the necessary arrangements now.*

This may have freaked you out a bit if you hadn't even considered throwing a party to welcome your book into the world. No matter how you're feeling about planning a book launch party, here's the most important thing to remember:

**It's your book launch party.**

There are no "right" or "wrong" ways to plan your book launch party. In fact, you may decide at the last minute to text your ten best friends and invite them to your house to celebrate your huge accomplishment. Or you may feel a book launch party is too overwhelming, like I did when I completed my first book, but your closest friends decide a celebration is in order and they make it happen.

If you want to plan a book launch party, which I really hope you do, the last step in Milestone 7 will help you prepare a "swag" item or two: pens, notebooks, bookmarks - any useful item you can surprise your book launch party guests with. *By the way, did you know "swag" means "stuff we all get"?*

**Note:** Pens are the top swag item, meaning they are the most useful and are kept longer than any other swag item. And if you're tapped out financially, I have excellent news: you can get custom made pens for under $2 a piece from my lovely friend Shannon Dyck at shannondesigns.ca.

Depending on your book launch plan, you may not have any actual books for sale at your event. You might choose to do what I did for this book, which is described in the **BONUS Party Planning** chapter. **Spoiler alert:** no one got to take a book home from my launch party for *"It's Time To Write Your Damn Book, Woman!"*.

## If you are undecided about a book launch party...

Consider this: it's not about you.

A book launch party should be about celebrating the people who need your book, who are your niche people, and everyone who helped you bring your book to life.

### *"Why am I celebrating the people who need my book?"*

Great question. It's because they are the reason you get to do what you love for a living. The people who come to your book launch party will be a mix of your past, present and future clients AND your biggest supporters. All of these people need to know they are appreciated and celebrated by YOU.

## A book launch party is not about making money

*...At least not in the short-term.* There will be a long-term ripple effect from your properly marketed book launch party

resulting in more income for you, but focus on using this instead:

**Use this rare event to spice up your marketing.**

How many other businesses in your industry will use a book launch party to attract their ideal clients in the next 1-2 years? How many book launch parties have you been invited to in the past 5 years? My point is, *it's still unique to write a book,* even though it has become more common in recent years.

## *"Do I need a second Instagram account?"*

If you have a personal Instagram account, please do not start a second Instagram account. Use your personal Instagram account to promote your new book and continue sharing highlights from your life like you used to. When you announce you are writing a book it's time to update your Instagram bio: add details about your upcoming book and links to your survey and website, if you have one.

Later you may see a real need for having two Instagram accounts, but unless there is a clear and important reason, don't add to your already long to-do list. Feeling like you have to post on two Instagram accounts is not fun. Plus it's not fun to start a new business/Author Instagram account with zero followers. It would be better to start a new personal account and switch your original account which has more followers into a business/Author account.

# Chapter 7:
## Edit, beautify & STOP

This is going to be the shortest chapter of the book! You are SO DAMN CLOSE to being an Author, woman - way to go!

## Formatting your book

After reading the suggestions made by your editors, and making any necessary changes to your book, it's time to change the *format* of your book from Google Docs to a version that can be printed and bound into a beautiful book.

I probably should have mentioned this earlier, but *you can upload a new copy of your manuscript to Amazon any time you want to.* This means that if you find a mistake in your book, you can fix it easily. Knowing I can make changes stops me from nit-picking my book to death.

When you are copying and pasting your writing from Docs into the KDP template, pay attention to text or images that are outside the margins. Even though you can upload a new manuscript PDF whenever you want, it still has to be *approved,* or it can't be printed. If the format of your book is not printable for any reason, KDP will send you an email saying it has been rejected and the reason why.

I show you in a video how I do all the formatting things at yycfempreneurs.com/author. My video walks you through choosing your book size, downloading the template from kdp.amazon.com, designing the layout, and uploading your cover design and manuscript PDF to Amazon.

**Reminder:** the videos at yycfempreneurs.com/author are worth over $1000! Take advantage - make sure you watch all of them!

## Layout: Mix it up, but stay consistent

This is easier to explain in a video while showing you what I mean. So I did explain it in the formatting video at yycfempreneurs.com/author. I'll do my best to explain it here too: the *layout* is the way your book's pages look. When designing the layout, **try to mix it up**. Rather than see page after page of writing in the exact same font, add bold headings, tables, graphs and images to look at. Don't bore them.

Here are examples of ways to mix up your layout:

- Choose one font for headings, another font for quotes, and a third font for chapter titles. One of these fonts can also be the main font.

- Add photos from your life to the stories you share.

- Use checklists and bullet points to present information rather than in paragraphs.

You'll notice I've done this in these pages to keep you from getting bored of pages that all look the same. However, I also made sure to **stay consistent** by using the same font throughout for body text, headings and chapter titles.

## How did you handle the editors' feedback?

As you read the *constructive criticism* provided by your editors, and when you see the red ink throughout the pages of your first draft book, there's only one thing that matters: completing the steps and crossing the finish line.

Done is better than perfect.

You're almost there.

Conversely, be careful not to lose yourself in the idea of becoming a full-time writer. You may be feeling really confident in your ability to write and market books right now, perhaps imagining how your "Author" status could pay all your bills…

## "Author": A viable career?

Probably not. I hate to be a downer, but if you are dreaming of a career as a "Published Author", it's likely you'll need other income streams. Most Authors can't live off just writing.

Many have side gigs like teaching. Plus most writers don't make it past *the gatekeepers of the traditional publishing world.* I'm not saying you should give up your dream of a big publisher like Penguin Random House buying your book manuscript and turning your masterpiece into a Netflix series. I daydream from time to time about writing a real page-turner that becomes a bestseller and TV series.

In the pre-tech world, the Steven Kings and Margaret Atwood made more money than they do today. Creating a printed book was more difficult and rare, which made it more profitable. Pre-tech book marketing channels were also narrower and fewer.

If you have researched the traditional publishing world, then you know it comes with as many restraints as financial benefits for the less than .01% of writers who make it past the gatekeepers. I'd rather keep writing books and choosing every word, image and book cover design by being a self-published Author. After all, we're all "Authors", even if our books don't make us rich or famous.

My goal was to become an Author. Once I was an Author, my goal became to continue writing books to share my knowledge until the day I die.

Why?

Because my mission is to help as many women as possible know the feelings and benefits that come from becoming an Author. I am very grateful that Amazon got on the "Print On Demand" bandwagon in 2016, the same year I self-published my first book. *Talk about impeccable timing!*

## The history of *self-publishing* and Print-On-Demand (POD)

Prior to POD, self-published Authors had to take the risk of bearing the costs of printing up-front, without knowing how many copies of their book (if any) would sell. With POD, a book is only printed when it is purchased, so Authors don't have to worry about printing more than they sell.

Thankfully in 1997, Lightning Source, one of the largest POD companies, was founded.

By 1999, blog hosting services like Blogger, LiveJournal, and WordPress were making it easier than ever for Authors to share their writing with the world. This led to a few of the top bloggers being offered book and movie deals.

Then came the first ebook reader released by Sony in 2004, and a few years later Amazon released the Kindle eReader. Of course it was linked to a huge online store full of ebooks and a monthly subscription... CHA-CHING!

Then Amazon launched Kindle Direct Publishing for ebooks, followed in 2016 by a POD paperback option.

My point in sharing this brief history lesson with you is the days of needing a publisher to print and market your book are over. Sure, it's nice to have the option to sell your book manuscript (and the rights to all your work) to a publisher for $10,000-$100,000, but it's not *necessary.*

You will get to add "Author" to your current list of professional roles no matter how many people buy your book, or how many book stores put your book on their shelves.

You are not a "lesser-Author" because you did all the work yourself and didn't wait through years of rejection letters before a friend-of-a-friend got your book noticed by a big publisher.

## You have full control of your book

Maybe you've sent your manuscript to a dozen publishers only to receive a few rejection letters and crickets from the rest. Maybe you're not going to quit trying until your book has been accepted by a traditional publisher, even though it could mean <u>you paying them to publish your book</u>, rather than the other way around.

If you're OK with handing over ownership of your book to a publisher, giving your creation to them to control...

**May I ask WHY?**

Why do you want to give control over the culmination of 100 -1000 hours of your time and effort, not counting the sleepless nights and daydreaming about what you want to say in your book, to someone other than yourself?

I'm not saying you shouldn't do it. I am not you, so I am not trying to steer you in any direction. I want you to understand what motivates you to write.

If your answer is money, that's fair. Depending on how much money they want to pay me, and what the contract looks like, I might even consider accepting a book deal from a well-known publisher.

If the reason why you would hand over your book has anything to do with getting your book on the shelf in big bookstores, or marketing your book online, know that you can do both of these things yourself. If you want to have your book for sale in stores, take copies of your book to the stores and ask to talk to a manager about selling your book in their store. Here in the Calgary area the Indigo stores have been very supportive of both myself and Tiana by agreeing to put our books in their stores. All you gotta do is ask!

## Old-school marketing

Marketing is always evolving, but the old-school methods will never change. Flyers on a few grocery store and coffee shop billboards are often as effective as boosting an Instagram post.

There will always be new and better ways to spread the word about a new book, product or service we have to offer. Keep repeating the marketing steps in this book so that the only person who could "drop the ball" on your marketing is YOU.

You decide:

◆ *how to spread the word about your book*

◆ **what to charge for it**

◆ **how many different ways you want to repurpose the knowledge in your book**

◆ **whether or not to record an audio version or ebook**

Do you want to turn your book into a course or workshop series? Do you want to give a free PDF version of the first three chapters to your new email subscribers? You decide because you created it and you own 100% of the rights to do what you want with it!

## Stay focused on what you stand for

Marketing is all about building relationships. Your book will be your best marketing tool if you stay focused on how it will help others. They will hear your loud and clear message: I am here to help you!

You wouldn't want to write or read a book that's full of sales pitches and reasons why readers need to *Buy Now!* Don't allow your own financial goals to damage your book's ability to build relationships. I did not write books with an expectation that they would make me more money. I stayed focused on creating books that will help women become more successful and guess what? *I became more successful from increased credibility and community growth.*

I wanted the credibility boost that would come from writing each book, but <u>that's not why I finished any of those books.</u>

What brought my books across the finish line, this one included, is picturing all of you reading these words:

*You can do this. You now have all the steps. Success is within your grasp, and I'm here to help you if you feel confused, or you need accountability.*

Remember when you pictured five people reading the last page of your book? How do you want them to feel about their new skills and knowledge? How do you want them to feel about you? Add to your goal board anything else you want them to understand and feel in their soul as they read the last page of your book.


## Know when to STOP

*I'm repeating this story, which I shared with you at the beginning of the book:*

When I was almost done writing my first book, I was shocked when I went back and read the first chapter. It had been a few months since I had written the first chapter and my writing had improved so much! I was excited, but also frustrated because I ended up re-writing the entire first chapter, which was time I wanted to put into layout and formatting. I fell a little more behind schedule when I saw the second chapter also needed more work!

Thank God for the Tim Ferriss Show Podcast episode I heard around that time: Tim said I needed to STOP. Just stop reading and making changes to my book and *hand it over to the editors.* But once I had their feedback, and implemented their changes, I found myself making <u>more</u> changes.

Having a book launch party scheduled will help you avoid **the mistake of not knowing when to STOP**. Having a book launch party has been a priceless part of the book writing process for me because I have to stick to a deadline. I have to STOP nitpicking and making changes to my writing.

In conclusion, when I decided my book was DONE, more of my precious time was invested in getting the book noticed by those who need it rather than nit-picking it to death.

## This is why I continue to write books:

Each book I've written has made me better at my most important roles: mother, daughter and friend, and allowed me to connect with many of the fabulous women who read my books.

Thanks for helping me connect with more fabulous women like you by gifting a copy of this book to a friend or family member who should write a book.

# BONUS CHAPTER:

# Party Planning

## Ways to use your book launch party as the ULTIMATE LEAD MAGNET

⭐ Eventbrite - help yourself and your book get discovered by people who don't know you by publishing your event on eventbrite.com.

Eventbrite charges a fee to use their platform, which is well worth the money because eventbrite events have high findability on Google, which means more people finding YOU.

**Eventbrite tip:** Do not choose to pass the fee on to your attendees. Always choose to *absorb the fees.* Price your event accordingly to cover the fee. If you do not choose to absorb the fee, the fee will show up as an additional charge when people are purchasing tickets, which will turn most people off. I feel it's unprofessional to show our clients the fees we pay to do business and ask them to pay the fees directly. They are busy and it is our job to help them take the right action as quickly as possible with no distractions.

Offering your event on your website can't compare to the discoverability of the world's largest event marketplace, eventbrite.com. They didn't pay me to say that.

☆ Live Video - ask your door prize donors and book editors to hop on a live video to chat about one of the topics in your book and help spread the word about your party and new book.

▷ *Your weekly marketing checklist includes **live video** because it's an extremely simple and valuable way to connect with more of the right people while wearing sweatpants.*

☆ Swag Bags - invite your business owner attendees to bring items for the swag bags, even if it's just a business card. You can do this by **asking the question on the next page on your ticket purchase form:**

## Contact information

✉ email@example.com

📞 (506) 234-5678                                               ⓘ

## Please list any food allergies:

Optional

## Swag bag items and/or a door prize:

✓ I will bring 20 swag bag items and a door prize

I will bring swag bag items only

I will bring a door prize only

Neither

## Card information

1234 1234 1234 1234                                    VISA ⬤ 🟦 JCB

MM / YY                               CVC                      ⬛

⭐ **Door Prizes** - the business owners who donate door prizes are more likely to share your event on their social media channels if you put their logo on the bottom of the event image under "Door Prize Sponsors". Or you can build an image like this at canva.com for each door prize that's donated:

A template for this image is available at
yycfempreneurs.com/author.

> ▷ *If you don't feel comfortable asking local businesses to <u>donate</u> door prizes, perhaps use $200 of your book launch budget to buy items from local businesses for a few gift baskets. When you pop into the shops, make sure to document your shopping trip (record videos of you opening the door, walking in, point the camera at your face and look excited, etc). Post your shopping videos and photos of the items you bought on social media and tag the store. On Instagram, you tag a store/account in your stories by tapping the sticker at the top and then @MENTION.*

## Unveiling your first *book selfie*

When you post your *book selfie* on social media, you want 2 things to happen:

1. People buy your book on Amazon IF they cannot attend your book launch party

2. People buy tickets to your book launch party

People who want the book and live near you will hopefully choose option 1. Anyone who can't attend your party (or doesn't like parties), will choose option 2.

This means that you need to <u>alternate between these two links</u> when posting your *book selfie* online: your Amazon book link and the party ticket link.

## Now let's imagine it's the BIG NIGHT...

Imagine people are starting to arrive at your book launch party. They see 5 or 6 copies of your book on a table, so they're curious: where's my book?

You politely let them know your book is on sale for 2 days only for half price. You direct them to the book table where they can hold a copy of your book in their hands. On the table there is a framed image of your book with a QR code that says "BUY NOW FOR HALF PRICE!"

Your guests scan the QR code with their cell phones and buy the book on Amazon because you explained to them the importance of **verified reviews**.

## My fourth book launch party

The **first party** wasn't really supposed to be a party. It was my first ever book signing at an Indigo store in Calgary which ended up feeling like a party. It was one of the best days of my life. So many people stopped by to see me and meet my new book baby. Many brought me flowers and gifts. It felt more like a baby shower!

At the time, I was not the avid party planner I am now. The idea of a book launch party stressed me out because I thought it had to be elaborate and expensive. I was not willing to take on any financial risk. I was happy my book was done, and I got to have an unexpected bonus party at an Indigo store.

Between my first and second book I became more savvy with planning parties from building the YYC Fempreneurs Community for over a year. Plus I had gained a team of like-minded women who contributed to my second book, *Find Your Voice on Social Media.* None of them had contributed to a book before, or wrote their own books, so they were stoked about the whole thing. I continually reminded everyone when I talked about the book and launch event: *"This event is not about me. It's about celebrating our team's success and the women whose participation in Fempreneur Marketing School inspired me to write the book."*

All seven women who contributed to the book did a great job marketing the event, and all of them did at least one Instagram Live to talk about their story in the book and the event. It was a true team effort.

At the event they each gave a speech and we had a fabulous evening celebrating with the 45 people who attended at a local brewpub. I charged $25 for tickets, which included a copy of the book, an appy buffet and one drink. I gave tickets to a handful of my financial clients and my book contributors, so about half the tickets were paid for. My out-of-pocket investment ended up being about $800. This was an excellent investment in my business. We are still feeling the ripple effect that started that night.

Each attendee received a copy of the book, which was included in the ticket price. These books were *author copies* ordered from <u>kdp.amazon.com</u>. Although author copies are quite inexpensive, usually $3-4 per book, they take FOREVER to arrive. That's one of the two reasons why I don't recommend ordering author copies as part of your book launch plan.

The other reason why you don't need author copies to successfully launch your book is in the rest of my story...

My third book launch party was more expensive, both because less people attended (it was 2021), and because the venue had a larger minimum spend. The minimum spend to have the room to ourselves was $1500. I had ordered about $600 in appetizers for my guests, who all paid $35 each to attend. During the event they collectively spent about $400 on other food and drinks. At the end of the night I bought $500 in gift cards to make up the rest of the minimum spend. My total investment was about $1000.

**None of the three book launch events I just described resulted in many people buying books on Amazon.** This is something I decided to change when I launched the book you are holding in your hands right now.

**Verified reviews** on Amazon are important to help your book get discovered by more people who need it. A verified review happens only when someone who buys an item on Amazon reviews it. For example, I can review a book I haven't bought on Amazon, but my review won't say "Verified Purchase", like this.

Only verified reviews count towards the overall rating of the book.

For the launch of this book, everyone arrived at my party and saw 5 copies of the book on a table. They were curious: where's my book? Next to the books they saw an image in a frame that said, *HALF PRICE ends in one week!* with a QR code. It was a Thursday night, by the way. While welcoming my guests, I explained how verified reviews work and asked them to *please purchase my book tonight for half price on*

*Amazon.* Then I asked them to help me spread the word about my new book until the half price sale ended.

This is exactly what I want you to do, plus I want to buy a copy of your book on Amazon when it is released! Don't forget to send me the link to buy a copy!

I'd love to come to your launch party too!

## I hope this has been helpful

If you have any questions, or you want to write your book alongside a team of other FemAuthors, send me a message at yycfempreneurs.com/contact :)

No matter what anyone tells you, or what happens in your life to throw you off course, YOU CAN DO THIS.

AND YOUR LIFE WILL BE BETTER WHEN YOU ARE AN AUTHOR.


~ Lyndsie Barrie

Lyndsie with FemAuthors Noreen Music and Felicia Yap.

## ABOUT THE AUTHOR

Lyndsie has been an instrumental part of turning mere ideas into viable businesses for many women entrepreneurs.

In 2019 Lyndsie launched a marketing school and community called YYC Fempreneurs. She has gone to the next level with publishing six books educating women.

Lyndsie tirelessly shares her passion for social media marketing and promotes collaboration with like-minded women through online workshops and live events in the Calgary area.

Hundreds of women have found the direction, confidence and connections they need to succeed thanks to Lyndsie and her community of Fempreneurs.

Lyndsie enjoys *me time* in the middle of nowhere swimming in a creek with her dog, sitting by a campfire sipping a cold beer, hiking or mountain biking. She loves watching her son play football and hockey. On most afternoons she can be found taking a 20 minute nap.

Manufactured by Amazon.ca
Bolton, ON